D0210226

A Special Gift for You

To ....

From ....

Message ....

....

....

....

Date ....

The Ego and the Spirit

The Ego and the Spirit

*Insights on Living,
Loving & Letting Go*

Fran Hewitt

Health Communications, Inc.
Deerfield Beach, Florida

www.hcibooks.com

To preserve confidentiality, various names have been changed in this manuscript.

**Library of Congress Cataloging-in-Publication Data
is available through the Library of Congress**

© 2017 Fran Hewitt

ISBN-13: 978-07573-1999-0 (Paperback)
ISBN-10: 07573-1999-8 (Paperback)
ISBN-13: 978-07573-2000-2 (ePub)
ISBN-10: 07573-2000-7 (ePub)

All rights reserved. Printed in the United States of America. No part of this publication may be reproduced, stored in a retrieval system, or transmitted in any form or by any means, electronic, mechanical, photocopying, recording, or otherwise, without the written permission of the publisher.

HCI, its logos, and marks are trademarks of Health Communications, Inc.

Publisher: Health Communications, Inc.
     3201 S.W. 15th Street
     Deerfield Beach, FL 33442–8190

*Cover design and inside text design/layout by Brandwithin, Phoenix, Arizona. Brandwithin.com
Cover photo by Donghan Lee*

I dedicate this book to you Dad

— I miss you —

Contents

Introduction

Have you ever been faced with a decision when your head says one thing and your heart says another? For example, you want to make a career change; your head tells you to follow the path of security, but your heart tells you to follow your passion. Or you are locked in a personal relationship conflict and your head says you are right, but your heart tells you to forgive and let go. It happens to me too. I call these two conflicting influences the Ego and the Spirit.

The Ego and the Spirit is not about religion or philosophy; in fact, it's a simple, profound book about living fully, loving freely, and letting go. In these pages, you'll discover 35 authentic snapshots of life that will entertain, enlighten, and challenge you to think about your own life experiences. Some of these vignettes are poignant, others are funny, and some will challenge you with thought-provoking questions. You will relate to many of these situations and hopefully find the content a springboard for stimulating discussion. As you read the chapters, many of which are personal, you'll witness the daily struggle between Ego and Spirit.

The Ego is that controlling voice of your mind that drives you to seek safety, perfection, and the approval of others. Like a taskmaster, its demands are constant— be nice, look good, don't make mistakes. Many women relate to this pressure for perfection and approval but do not recognize their Ego's influence behind it. Unfortunately, unless you recognize and master your Ego's desire to control your every choice, it will keep you captive. In the chapters "The Masks We Wear" and "Too Nice for Your Own Good" you'll witness the manipulative power of the Ego.

In contrast, the voice of your Spirit is that reassuring voice that insists, urges, and shows you the way to love. It's the voice of your heart. The Spirit is a call to live life without fear and to trust in its guidance. When you live in harmony with your Spirit, you'll discover a new level of creativity, healthier and more loving relationships, and the freedom to be authentic. The results of listening to your Spirit instead of to the louder voice of your Ego will be obvious and sometimes instantaneous. You will know with certainty that your life is richer and more meaningful.

In my early years growing up in Ireland, my Ego was my protector, but as I grew older its need for control got in the way of how I wanted to live. Today, as you will discover, I much prefer to listen to my Spirit.

When I chose to follow my heart to write this book, I was choosing to follow the voice of my Spirit. There was a creative energy wanting to pour out of me onto these pages. If I had chosen to follow my head instead, I would have been listening to the voice of my Ego, urging me to seek the security of a paycheck or some new business activity. Usually when I listen to my heart, good things happen and *The Ego and the Spirit* is the result. This little book is packed full of life experience and has the power to make a difference to your life.

Maybe you'll be inspired to make some exciting changes, decide to live life more fully, or learn not to take the same ill-conceived path that I did. Perhaps you will awaken to the power of your own Spirit by consistently asking, "My Ego says this ... but what does my Spirit say?" By choosing to follow your Spirit's guidance more often you will liberate your life.

No matter what age or stage of life you are at there is a gift waiting for you within these pages. My wish is that you'll find it and use it for your greatest benefit.

I respectfully offer *The Ego and the Spirit* as a gift from my life to yours.

— Fran Hewitt

1

The Surrender

For many years I found it challenging to purchase a card for Father's Day. I would stand and scan the rack for ages, looking for something—anything—that would truthfully fit my relationship with my dad. Most of the cards were either too gushy—*You're the best dad in the world*—or simply untrue—*You were always there for me.* The words other people bought to express their love reminded me year after year of how different my relationship with my father was. It

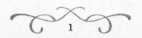

was guarded, conflicted, and challenging at best.

I usually settled for a silly card; it was safe and Dad was always good with humor.

His sense of fun had served him well before his life began to erode, before his body stopped co-operating and dementia clouded his reality. In fact, on his 78th birthday Dad bought himself a new Mini Cooper. It was his pride and joy. He loved that little car and all the attention that came with it. Wearing his black leather jacket and racing cap, he'd go whizzing around the neighborhood. My father lived to drive!

But three years later, Dad suffered from a serious debilitating illness that revealed a failing mind and forced him to move into a nursing home. Worse, his driver's license was revoked. In a matter of minutes, the authorities snatched away his independence and robbed him of his reason to live. Losing his license was no laughing matter. It was the beginning of the end.

On admission day Dad stubbornly left his walker at the door and walked around the nursing home unassisted. That's my dad! That first day he played the piano, chatted with some residents, and winked and smiled and sang. That's my dad! I breathed a sigh of relief; he was going to be all right. But the next day, as if in a sit-down protest, he plunked himself into a wheelchair, never to walk again. "I want to go home now," he declared. My heart broke. That's my dad!

Taking care of my father in his last years was tough in every way. I was exhausted physically and emotionally. I juggled my busy life around his care. In a desperate attempt to make things easier for him, I tried to soak up his pain and frustration like a sponge, denying my own feelings of resentment and guilt. To cope, I kept myself focused on the practical issues of his care. This was more comfortable than having to sit, chat, and visit. I meted out my time with him and rationed how much I was willing to give. Although my

Spirit wanted me to engage at a deeper level, my Ego kept me disconnected. I didn't want to see his pain or feel his helplessness. I needed him to be happy *for my sake*; but he hated his life and I dreaded our visits.

Then something changed in both of us. One day when he was particularly lucid, he asked me, "Where did my old life go?" In that moment of vulnerability both our shells seemed to crack. I felt my hardened heart begin to break,

Spirit wants us to engage with others at a deeper level.

then soften. Love and compassion replaced the anger I'd known most of my life for my father. His vulnerability had triggered in me a surrender to everything that our relationship had been and what it could become.

My father started using words like gratitude and love—I nearly fell off my chair in shock! This new Dad was softer; he seemed more approachable. He too

seemed to have surrendered—to his helplessness and the reality of his situation. He started to joke again and welcomed me on each visit with a delighted grin.

A lot of healing happened under the bright fluorescent lights of the nursing home cafeteria. I started to enjoy being with him. On his good days we would sit, chat, laugh, and be together. When the warm weather beckoned beyond the windows, I would wheel his chair into the garden and we would silently watch the birds together. He would hold onto my hand. "Don't go yet!" he'd plead. Now that he's gone, I wish I'd stayed longer.

I bought a Father's Day card just a week before he passed away. It still took me ages to choose because now I had too many loving verses to pick from.

I love you, Dad, and I miss you.

MY **EGO** SAYS
*"I need to protect
my heart from you."*

MY *Spirit* SAYS
*"My heart needs
no protection,
I love you freely."*

2

The Masks We Wear

One of the wonderful advantages of getting older is that I'm finally growing into my own skin. I now understand what it means to honor my true self and to live authentically. But for years, hiding behind masks and pretending to be somebody else was more important to me than being true to myself. I was scared to be me.

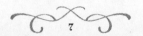

Early on in life I realized that fitting in was safer than being unique. Like many young women I wanted my peers to accept me. I laughed when they laughed and mimicked them in every way. I pretended to like certain boys they thought were drop-dead gorgeous— even though I saw only pimple-faced nerds. I made up stories about my escapades on the weekends so they'd think I was cool—even though my weekends were as dull as dishwater, spent babysitting my younger siblings and never going anywhere. I was terrified of being ostracized, so, like a puppet on a string, I allowed everyone to manipulate me. I cared more about what others thought of me than about what I thought of myself. But deep down inside, I knew I was a fraud.

I know many others have felt this same fear. Many people feel a huge disparity between who they *are* and who they think they *should* be. We believe we constantly need to improve ourselves, so we put on our masks to cover up. We disguise our weaknesses, hide our flaws, and bury those things that make us unique—because we believe that's what we have to do to fit in.

Many women have used their masks so often and for so long that they no longer have any true sense of self. Instead of being unique individuals, living from their truth, they hide in the safety of their disguises, presenting only a shadow of themselves to others. One woman I know couldn't even tell her closest friends for a whole year that she had been divorced—she was terrified of presenting herself to the world as anything other than a married woman.

Ego can keep us blinded to all the ways that we cover up.

What makes us unable to show our true selves? Fear! It's less terrifying to buy someone's approval than to face rejection. It's nicer to please someone than to disappoint. It's easier to play peacekeeper than to face conflict even when we know it's better to speak up. It's easier to play the victim than to face up to our responsibility. But these fears and excuses keep us hidden behind our masks, scared to show the world who we really are and what we're capable of doing.

When I became a mother and held my first baby in my arms, I felt inadequate. I wanted my beautiful daughter to grow up with confidence and to value her uniqueness. But how was I to be a mentor when I didn't have a clue who I was or how to acquire these qualities for myself?

That was a turning point. I became a voracious reader, practically inhaling every self-help book I could get my hands on. I plucked up the courage to attend personal-growth workshops and even went for counseling. For the first time, I began to understand who *I* was, what it meant to be real, and to find the courage to be myself.

One day I realized how far I had come in this journey of authenticity. I had been chosen to be part of a team

to help my mentor in an intensive-healing workshop. He wanted me to work with one of the participants in front of the entire group. I revered this man. I wanted to please him and make him think I was great. It was tempting to show off my skills and wow everyone with a dazzling "performance."

Instead, I allowed myself to be vulnerable, and I realized I only needed to be myself, not some star seeking applause. My heart opened to the participant; my Spirit spoke freely, and I focused on staying present and authentic. My life force and my real self met each other for the first time, and everything changed for me that day. If only I had known sooner how absolutely fabulous I am!

Many women relate to this topic of wearing masks and strive to live more authentically. It doesn't happen overnight; it takes a conscious effort and often years of self-observation to discover what's not true about yourself. Of course, your Ego will attempt to keep you blinded to all the ways you cover up because it has a vested interest to stay in control.

If you're tired of erasing yourself and ignoring your own needs due to serving everyone else – stop! Starting today, make a conscious choice to be real in every situation that you face. Remember to have compassion for the frightened, needy version of yourself who may still, on occasion, fall back into old patterns. If you catch yourself in the act of putting on your masks, just smile. After all, it takes time to change old habits.

My life is more like a peep show now. I will pull out my best to show you but I will also reveal my not-so-great side— warts and all. If you run away or reject me, I might feel vulnerable or hurt for a minute or two because I'm still sensitive to rejection, but I have finally realized that it's not your job to like or respect me, it's mine.

Just to fit in, we bury those things that make us unique.

Keeping up these charades is exhausting. Consider how much stronger you would be if, instead of using your energy to keep your masks in place, you used it to uplift, validate, and invigorate yourself.

Make daily choices to be who you really are. Don't sell yourself out for anyone or anything.

MY EGO SAYS
"I wear a mask to feel accepted and loved."

MY *Spirit* SAYS
"I am worthy of being accepted and loved."

3

Living in the Gap

I regained consciousness in the hospital theatre. I
was groggy from the remnants of the anesthetic and
my eyes remained closed but I was cognizant enough
to hear sounds. A nurse placed a warm blanket over
my body and said, "We'll be admitting Mrs. Hewitt to
32 B." I wanted to alert her, "You've made a mistake,
this was only a biopsy, I'm going home to my children,
they're waiting for me," but my tongue felt like
lead and I couldn't form the words. As they pushed

my gurney down the hall I heard a sob. Why was my husband crying? At 33 years of age I had lost my health.

Before my diagnosis of advanced breast cancer I had been a gap dweller. I played the "when … then" game. When the children are older, then … When I get my career back in focus, then … When we move to a bigger home, then … I was always putting my life on hold.

Why is there always a gap between what we have and what we want? Is it a human trait or a North American affliction to negate, ignore, and minimize what we have? Why is it so difficult to be content?

Take advertising, for one thing. Have you noticed the way clever advertising ignites our flames of dissatisfaction? We are seduced by media myths. We are convinced the media have the answers to looking younger, being happier, and becoming irresistible to hunks in bars!

Voices louder than our own trick us into believing that the answers to happiness are elsewhere—anywhere but where we are now. When we invalidate where we are, we cannot feel delight in each day because we are unable to focus on it, or even see it. Instead, we focus on the gap and believe the grass is greener somewhere else.

We do not see the joy in our lives because we are not taught to focus on it. Instead, we are taught to focus on our discontent.

I now realize that loss is one of the great anchors of life. It is often through our losses that we can finally comprehend what

Why is there always a gap between what we have and what we want?

we have and, perhaps too late, what we've lost. We lose our jobs and wish we hadn't been so reckless in our spending. We lose our health and realize our well-being is vital to everything. We lose someone close and notice how much we took that person for granted. It's only when we experience loss that most of us finally wake up to what we had all along.

One of the many gifts of my prognosis was eradicating the gap from my life. A new me was born from that crisis. My eyes were opened to what really mattered, and with a new perspective I saw each day for the precious gift it was. I unwrapped each moment as it came, and my heart was grateful for everything

Through our losses we finally waken up to what we had all along.

I had. Despite my supposed sooner than later expiry date, I was determined to see my babies grow up, and I fought hard to stay encouraged through my treatments. I finally realized through it all that life is a journey, not a destination, and that living in the gap is a choice.

Life is now, not at some future place in time. Every day you can choose how you want to live it. You can choose to focus on what's lacking or choose to appreciate all of the gifts that you already possess.

As you may have surmised, I have long since outlived my expiry date. I'm much too busy living to die anytime soon!

MY EGO SAYS

"I won't be content until..."

MY *Spirit* SAYS

"I'm content."

4

Driven to Distraction

*E*veryday habits ingrained into our routines are often a comfort to us because we can be marvelously unconscious when we engage in them. Take a typical morning, for example; we can shower, brush our teeth, and get to work without even waking up. This is a blissful relief from the constant pressure of needing to be alert and focused. But what about those little habits, those niggling things we do, that can drive someone else to distraction?

I have been married for 33 years. That's a long time to live with anyone. I know I'm a saint! But whether you've been in a relationship for three months or thirty-three years, sharing the same space, the same bathroom, and the same bed comes with challenging compromises. Okay, your partner's habits may be minor irritations and not nuclear disasters; depending on your mood, they can be hilarious or hurtful.

Take my husband, Les, for example. He's a pretty steady guy and likes the same old breakfast every morning. For slicing his

Depending on your mood those quirks can be hilarious or hurtful.

banana he covets a special knife and he's warned me—hands off. But a knife is a knife, and if it's handy, I'll use it to spread my peanut butter on my toast or slice a tasty piece of cheddar for my omelet. He goes berserk, especially if I don't clean it afterward. He's peeved that I had the gall to actually use his knife. He's now hiding his banana-slicing knife from me.

Of all the ways he bugs me, however, one of my biggest peeves is his preoccupation with towels. No matter how often I complain, explain, or attempt to discipline his wayward ways, he will not yield. He refuses to dry his hands on the towel that's available; instead, he sneaks a clean one off the shelf in the bathroom, uses it, folds it and puts it back! This unhinges me! With my eagle eyes I can tell when he's messed with my clean stack. For goodness sake—I'm the only other person living in the house; you'd think I had a communicable disease! He then adds insult to injury by messing with my bathroom color schemes. After a shower, he'll use the maroon towel from the other bathroom and leave it in the green bathroom, or vice versa. With my aesthetic sensibilities affronted, I confront him. He says he's sorry but within a week, there it is again. I sense a gladiatorial combat when it comes to his issue with towels, and he's not surrendering any time soon.

I thought I was perfect but my husband has a few pet peeves of his own. Like when I don't properly secure the lids on food containers. It's a risk for him to lift any jar out of the fridge; he's been baptized by the contents on more than one occasion. Reluctant to change my sloppy ways, I argue,

How we react to perceived transgressions is always a choice.

"Don't lift anything by the lid." Another gripe he has is when I pack every available inch of the garbage bag, so when he goes to lift it, stuff spills out everywhere.

I've heard women complain about toilet seats being left up, hair in the sink, and laundry on the floor. I'm sure you have your own list. When it comes to what's important, you need to sort out the rocks from the sand. How we react to these perceived transgressions is always a choice. When I'm in a good mood, I can make fun of the situation and laugh it off. But on days when I'm sleep deprived and dragging my irritation behind me—be warned!

Despite being weird about towels and obsessive about knives, my husband is a keeper. He has learned when to stand his ground and when to run for his life.

MY EGO SAYS

"Why do you continue to do that stuff? Don't I matter to you?"

MY *Spirit* SAYS

"It's all small stuff, and it doesn't matter."

5

Hidden Secrets

$\mathcal{B}$oth of my parents were private people. This was the norm for most families in the early years of my childhood. My parents insisted that family matters stayed in the family; it was our business, after all, no one else's. "What will the neighbors think?" was a common mantra. Limited by what was permitted and what was not, I learned how to be button-lipped about family matters and keep any dirty laundry hidden. The unconscious bonds of family loyalty

held us as tight as any clam.

One of my earliest memories of wanting to hide occurred when I was six years old. I was playing in the kitchen with two of my sisters. Dad stormed in and demanded, "Who scribbled on the wallpaper? Own up, now!" I wanted to disappear, as I was the guilty one. Dad was scary when he shouted. I knew it was a sin to lie and if I did, there would be a black smudge on my soul. So I reluctantly owned up and got a whipping.

As I got older and more cunning, I decided that black smudges were less painful than telling the truth. I became a skilled liar and even witnessed my siblings punished for my deeds. One of my sisters is still blackmailing me with guilt because of all the lickings she endured as a child on my behalf. I can handle her. It's the black smudges I'm worried about now! Sorry, sisters!

For many years after, when questioned directly by people in authority, a little voice would remind me it's not safe to tell the truth.

It takes energy to keep things hidden. Our secrets, shameful events, and past pain, when internalized, fester like open wounds. We are as sick as our secrets, and they can change who we are. When you hold onto a malignant secret, it can dominate your consciousness and cloud your happiness affecting

The unconscious bonds of family loyalty can hold us as tight as any clam.

your relationships in a negative way. Some people withdraw or become uncommunicative in an effort to avoid sharing what is burdening them. Others find it blocks their capacity for intimacy and connection. Fear and shame are often the motivations preventing us from uncovering a personal secret. "What will they think about me when I share this?" However, if kept concealed, secrets can not only harm you but also impair your closest relationships.

In one of my workshops, a courageous woman revealed that she'd had an extramarital affair. The relationship was over long ago but the secret was eating away at her. Her husband was unaware of her indiscretion; in fact, this disclosure was the first time she'd shared it with anyone. It was her belief that the burden of shame and guilt that she carried was affecting her fragile marriage.

Like an insistent memory, a secret wants to be noticed and verified.

Within the confines of that workshop she experienced immediate relief in disclosing her secret. Buoyed by the support and safety of the group, she gave herself permission to unburden her shame. I don't know if she chose to tell her husband or not, but the work she did that weekend started her healing.

In fact, the next time I met her I hardly recognized her. She looked ten years younger, radiant, and happy. It was the courage to disclose her secret that saved her marriage.

In my first book, *The Power of Focus for Women*, I revealed many personal life experiences. Some were deep emotional wounds and some were about my troubled relationship with my father. For me, writing the book was both a difficult and cathartic process but not everyone welcomed my frankness and honesty. People who preferred privacy were embarrassed because I had exposed my life to public scrutiny.

How do you discern what is harmful to keep hidden and what is safe to be revealed? This dilemma provokes your consciousness. Like an insistent memory, a secret wants to be noticed and verified. You may attempt to ignore it, rationalize it, or cover it with reproach, but it will just keep nagging you. There are issues that need to be brought into the light. But who do you disclose them to? Sometimes the matter is private and personal; sometimes we need someone to share our pain.

When you tell your secrets and unveil hidden burdens, you cannot always control the outcome. That raises other issues to consider. Do you speak up if keeping silent could cause harm? Yes. Is it necessary to disclose to someone if it will cause an irreparable rift? Perhaps not. Seek the help of a professional when you're in doubt.

The more we can share our secrets and take responsibility for our healing, the less shame and power we carry around in our psyche. Discern the best and most loving way to set yourself free. Honor yourself and others in the process and drop any expectations that you might have. This takes courage and commitment.

What do you hide? And from whom do you hide it?

MY **EGO** SAYS
*"Keep quiet, and keep up
the image at all costs."*

MY *Spirit* SAYS
"Tell the truth."

6

It Never All Gets Done

My mind is up long before my body is willing to be. I go over the list one more time. Take the chicken out of the freezer; put in a load of laundry; swing by the bakery for a farmer's loaf on the way to work; pick up the parmesan cheese and lettuce on the way home ... It's now 6 a.m. and, as time waits for no man or multi-tasking woman, I drag my body out of bed; I'm up and off to the races.

I wash and fix my hair (note to self: book a salon appointment), walk the dog, add cereal to grocery list, pack lunches ... and after eight long hours of juggling pressures at work I'm still going like the Duracell battery. Call the renovator to pick up the tile; do my Spanish homework; take laundry out of the dryer.... I'm on a fast-paced treadmill, and if I don't keep moving I'll collapse in exhaustion or be buried alive under a huge mountain of to-dos. It's just a typical, cramming, juggling, dashing-about, hectic day.

Have you noticed how life can be unrelenting? We usually have too much to do and too little time to do it. It's little wonder we get cranky and freak out when anyone demands yet another piece of us. Seeking life balance has become the Holy Grail of frazzled women everywhere.

In our intrusive world, protecting and using our time wisely has never been more important. Yet with too many urgent tasks to attend to and not enough hours in a day, how can we ever get caught up? Voice mail messages demand a call back; critical emails cry out for a response; and unfinished business nags at our conscience whenever we take a break. Computer screens framed with yellow sticky notes blatantly remind us (lest we forget) just how busy we are.

Seeking life balance has become the Holy Grail of frazzled women everywhere.

Our busy lifestyles are not always to blame for the overload. When I ask women why they have so much on their plates, many of them answer that they did it to themselves. It was their choice to be busy; they confess to *deliberately* taking on too much. They admit to being addicted to the adrenaline rush and love the challenge of waiting until the last minute. Other women claim their value is tied to how busy they can be. Then there are those who are afraid to have time with themselves, not knowing how to be. They create drama and chaos to keep themselves distracted.

Have you ever turned your day inside out and upside down just because someone said the word *urgent?* I once read a quote that said, "Don't let someone else's urgency become your emergency."

How many times have I fallen for the tyrannical trickster called *Urgency?* Automatically I would feel compelled to dash about, squeeze in, stand on my head, and do whatever it took to calm the storm or put out the fire. I was seduced by the rush and too often lost sight of the fact that *urgent* doesn't always mean there's a fire.

I was especially vulnerable to my husband's cry of *urgent.* Les used to procrastinate a lot. (I do give him kudos for being much improved today.) Back then, the evening before a workshop, he would scrawl pages of indecipherable notes and announce that he needed them typed up for handouts. He had five weeks to produce these handouts and enough staff at the office to get them prepared. But no, he dillydallied and deferred, delaying the inevitable.

Enter the good wife to the rescue. Here I was at ten o'clock at night, the only typist in sight, looking at six pages of hieroglyphics. He knew I would always come through and bail him out. That was the pattern. He would procrastinate. I would rescue, all the while ranting, raving, and resenting that his tardiness had once again become my emergency. Chastened, he would promise that this was the very last time. Then one day I finally wised up and said NO! Even though he claimed that this time it was an exceptionally urgent matter with dire consequences. NO! I did not capitulate under the pressure. NO! My guilt tried to bury me; I buried it instead.

My gobsmacked husband soon learned that urgent fires can be prevented and I wasn't the fire brigade!

The question, "Does this *really* need to be done right now?" often stops me from strapping on my rollerblades and causes me to rethink my priorities. I gradually became aware that just because I liked to get things done meant I was choosing my own agenda for completion over more important things, such as relationships that needed my attention or a tired body that needed time for self-care. Be warned! If you ignore what's important, it may soon become urgent and you'll have another crisis to deal with.

> *There will always be something competing for your attention.*

So how do we decide what to do and what to leave out?

Here's a mantra that may save your sanity: *It never all gets done.* Isn't that true? There will always be something competing for your attention. Say this every day until it becomes embedded in your brain: *It never all gets done!*

When we know it never all gets done, learning to manage our time better helps us focus on completing our most important priorities. Multi-tasking can help us cover a lot of tasks, but when it comes to completing an important goal, doing too many things at once can distract and scatter our focus. Prioritizing and scheduling may be easier at work than at home; at work we're focused on deadlines and understand time lines better. The home and family front is often more difficult.

It helps to be clear on what you value most and to prioritize your time around these. Make a list of the major areas and rate them. Health, relationships, finances, freedom, career … For instance, if you value good health, you will want to prioritize time for preparing healthy meals over the faster, less healthy option of take-out. If you value free time with your family over making more money, you'll schedule your weekends off. It doesn't all get done anyway, so why not make sure life is done your way?

MY EGO SAYS
"I need to get it all done now."

MY *Spirit* SAYS
"It never all gets done, and that's okay."

7

The Shadow of Doubt

$\mathcal{I}$ used to be indecisive, but now I'm not sure.

I battled with self-doubt for years, especially when it related to my work. Was it good enough? Was I smart enough? Would anyone listen? I listened to the louder voices around me whom I believed to be worthier. They were the experts. They were the ones with the superior intellects and better ideas. I believed in them and negated anything that I had to offer. Then I realized that no one would listen to me until I first learned to listen to myself, my own voice, and my own truth.

Do you second-guess your own decisions and consistently listen to someone else's voice instead of your own? Do you believe that what you think, and who you are, isn't good enough? Is your self-esteem so battered that it seems impossible for you to ever believe in yourself?

Self-doubt is a by-product of low self-esteem and can also be a consequence of fear, such as the fear of making a mistake. In my early school days I was reminded daily that I was stupid. The teachers would cane me for the simplest mistakes, such as getting my spelling wrong. At home, instead of receiving encouragement and support, I was yelled at

Do you second-guess your own decisions?

for doing poorly at school. The belief that I was not good enough permeated my childhood.

When children grow up with shame they learn to move away from themselves. I moved so far that I no longer knew who I was. I was humiliated to be me. This was when I first went "missing."

I turned my back on a wonderful, creative, sensitive child who was beaten down by others. I left her shamed, alone, and discarded to fend for herself. Instead of being an independent, self-assured young woman, I grew into someone who defined herself by the approval and ideals of others, a pawn to everyone else's opinions. My motto was, "Tell me how you want me to be."

It takes courage to find your own voice and commit to staying true to yourself.

The journey back to find myself was long. I enrolled in courses that stretched my comfort zone and challenged my beliefs. I became a self-help junkie and read everything I could get my hands on. I sought counseling and woke up my wounded parts and cried out my hurts. Eventually I learned to shut out the voices that said I wasn't worthy. I discovered I had a return ticket to rescue my missing and abandoned self. I brought her home.

Is it possible to change your direction and destiny?

If a ship at sea can totally change course with only a two-degree shift in direction, you, too, can change your direction. Do it one day at a time, by reclaiming who you are and taking back your power. If you feel you have abdicated and abandoned yourself, identify when you first went missing. If you've been devalued and beaten down with lies, make a conscious decision to fight back. Your life has as much value as anyone else's. You are just as worthy. Focus on what you do well,

and you will find that your self-competence and self-confidence will develop as you build on your successes.

It's imperative to surround yourself with people who support your journey—your own personal cheerleaders. Banish all the voices that say, "You'll never do it." Or at least choose not to listen. Instead, seek out encouragers who will walk alongside you and help build your esteem as you learn to grow into yourself. Some people become their own cheerleaders because they are alone or they just don't have positive people to help them. My main supporter has always been my husband, Les. He has never doubted me.

It takes courage to find your own voice, to realize your worth, and to commit to staying true to yourself. There is a purpose for your life and a job to do while you're here. Without a doubt, it's *your* voice that needs to be heard and *your* life that needs to be lived.

MY EGO SAYS

"I doubt you have worth."

MY *Spirit* SAYS

*"I'm worthy,
no doubt about it!"*

8

The Thread that Connects Us All

*A*t the age of 14, life as I experienced it changed dramatically. A war that had been festering in Northern Ireland for some time finally erupted. "The Troubles" began as a war between political activists and paramilitary groups from both the Republican and Loyalist sides, but like many wars, it soon became one of religious division—Protestants against Catholics. Both sides claimed God as their own. But there was no God in this battle, only hatred and fear.

I feared for my family. A knock at the door at night would send us into panic. My father would yell for us to lie low while he, gun in hand, would check who was at the door. I held my breath and prayed it wasn't terrorists who'd come to shoot him. This war took the lives of thousands of civilians and maimed even more. It was a dangerous time of bombings and bullets. The tension at home was palpable. The radio and television were constant reminders of why we lived in fear. I'd listen to the blast of bombs at night as my world crumbled.

During this time I witnessed first hand the atrocities of war. Each day I risked my life getting to and from my work as an X-ray technician at a hospital in a dangerous location. I dodged bullets ricocheting off the hospital walls and risked being caught in an unexpected bomb blast. But somehow I learned to cope, stifling the horror of the chaos around me. Only after losing a friend to one of those bombs did I realize I had become completely numb.

I survived the war but not without scars. My wounds were not physical but emotional and spiritual. I had witnessed what separation could do when neighbor turned on neighbor. I decided I would never again accept God as a reason for division.

Despite the religious wars and differences that continue to be a part of our world, I believe a spiritual revolution is happening in people's lives. From the state of our environment to our fear of economic strife, there is a sense that something is dying—the old way of living. We are afraid to let go and yet it's imperative that we do. We can no longer ignore the fact that we're a global community; we're in this together. Our Earth struggles to sustain us. To save our lives and our planet—perhaps for the first time—we are finally awakening to our spiritual nature.

Spirit means breath. Spirit is the life force breathed into each of us. Spirit is the thread that connects all humanity, no matter what your religion. Spirit gives meaning to life.

We all have an inherent need to search for meaning and purpose. It's our raison d'être, for truly we are spiritual beings having a human experience. So it's sad that many people are so hurt and disillusioned by religion that they decide to ban spirituality from their lives altogether. I cannot imagine how devastating it would be to come to the end of my days and feel that my whole life had been for nothing. How would you feel if you never discovered your reason for being here?

We are finally awakening to our spiritual nature.

I want my life to have meaning and purpose, to be all used up at the end of my days. To stay on track and remain focused, I need continuous communication with my Spirit by taking the time to be quiet. In the busyness of life, I have found it's the only way I'm able to remain awake to my spiritual nature.

Are you willing to discover a greater meaning in life, the spiritual nature of your being? When you follow the urgings of your Spirit, not only will you find more meaning to life, but your eyes will also be opened to see that Spirit is everywhere—in others, in the beauty of nature, and in synchronicities that happen everyday. You will see Spirit at work in the miracles you witness, the earthly angels you meet, and in the grace you receive again and again. Perhaps when you pick up that spiritual thread that connects us all, you will feel a tug to join in the revolution. Not one of guns and bombs, but one of peace, love, and meaning.

MY **EGO** SAYS
"Without me you are nothing."

MY *Spirit* SAYS
"I am the true essence in everyone."

9

Are You a Missing Person?

I once had my own life, way back when I was a teenager. It may not have been pretty, however, it was my own. Then when I matured, married, and became a mother, my own life disappeared. It belonged to everyone else: my husband, my children, my boss, my elderly parents ... You get the picture. "Be all things to all people" was the pre-programmed mantra, and I chanted along with the sisterhood for many years. All those years of living

life to accommodate everyone else certainly had variety and its own rewards. The sacrifices I made resulted in a rather attractive glow of martyrdom. But where did I go in the meantime? That woman who had aspirations and dreams of her own?

Many believe that what they do is who they are.

"Missing in action" is a phrase I use to describe women who have lost touch with themselves. Mothers and caregivers are often victims to this.

I have also met women who disappear into their relationships. It's like they morph and melt into the "we." Togetherness becomes like a single-celled organism with no unique individuality evident. Other women are swallowed up by their careers, believing that what they do is who they are. It's a big challenge to keep your boundaries intact and stay true to who you really are.

As a young woman you have barely figured out what you want to be when you grow up, never mind having had the time to know yourself. Then you are suddenly launched into a world that tells you how you *should* be. You should be happy and satisfied while you balance the budget, birth your family, and bring home the bacon. In other words, you are supposed to suck it up, see it through, and keep quiet, at least until menopause. So if you've forgotten who you are, don't worry; at least owe it to yourself to get out alive!

There's more to life than being in someone's orbit.

When my children first left home I felt lost. I'd spent many years orbiting around their every need. I had worn my mother identity for so long that all I knew was to feel needed. Then soon after, Rafferty the family dog died and I didn't even have her around to nurture and love. I was lost in a void, spinning around without an identity.

"Who am I?" I asked myself. "What do I want?" The concept that there's more to life than being in someone's orbit was finally sinking in. I could have my own life at last! Instead of looking back and feeling that the good part was over, I was on a mission to look forward and find out what I was made of. Meanwhile my husband, who was delighted that all the competition for my attention had vanished, was scheming. "At last, she's all mine," he said with a glint in his eye. "You can orbit me now!"

That's when menopause hit—unfortunate timing for him!

MY EGO SAYS
"I am what I do."

MY *Spirit* SAYS
"I am more than you can imagine."

10

Comparison—a Game of Sabotage

*D*uring the first morning of my three-day workshop, I ask the participants to look around the room at the other people in the group. I then challenge them, "Have you already judged someone by the way they are dressed or by what they do for a living? Have you compared yourself to the others and do you feel superior or inferior to them?" We all laugh—of course they had!

My intention here is not to taunt but to teach. There are valuable lessons to be learned in this self-observation. However, it's not until our last day together that many of the women finally grasp these truths and begin to integrate them. Most of us compare ourselves, whether we do it consciously or unconsciously. Unfortunately, this can feed our insecurities and lead to alienation, even when we'd like to feel connected.

We may never measure up. Instead of winning, we'll be the biggest loser.

It's in our nature to compare and judge, especially for those of us who are competitive. We have our own scale of hierarchy for everything: intelligence, success, looks, material possessions, occupation.

Why do we continue to look at other people's strengths and compare them to our weaknesses? This sabotages our confidence and gives our flagging self-esteem an unnecessary downward jolt. It can lead to jealousy, insecurity, and self-hatred. Does it really matter that someone else has more than you? If you always want what others have, you will never have enough. We may never measure up. Instead of winning, we'll be the biggest loser.

We learn to compare at an early age. Being the second born in my family, it was inevitable that I wore hand-me-down clothes from my sister. It was a struggle for my parents to dress and feed six children. To get something new just for me was rare. Many of my playmates wore pretty dresses and had extra money to spend on treats. I felt poor. I remember comparing myself to the other students in my class. They were always smarter. I felt inadequate. This self-abuse and the feeling of being inferior to everyone else was automatic and ongoing.

My mother must have clued in, because one day she said to me, "There will always be girls smarter than you,

and there will also be girls not so smart. There will always be girls prettier than you, but there will also be some who are not as pretty." I never forgot her words, and I remember taking comfort in them. Unfortunately, even though I kept reminding myself of this truth, the pattern of self-abuse was deeply rooted and I continued to struggle with feelings of inferiority.

When I became a mother, feeling superior was a new way of building my fragile Ego. Instead of comparing myself and always being the lowest denominator, I was now going to flaunt my elevated status. After all, I believed I had the smartest and best-dressed children in the school. I was the puffed-up mother watching her children excel where I had not: I was living vicariously and precariously through them. This proud mum thing I had going on was really an absurd form of sabotage.

We don't realize how often we play this comparison game. By comparing ourselves to others and feeling superior, we're building a short-lived sense of security and confidence. When we measure ourselves as inferior, we feel insecure and erode our self-esteem. You can't win at this absurd game. In fact, you'll always lose.

Be more conscious of when and how often you play this game of sabotage. And don't beat yourself up when you catch yourself comparing; just notice what you are doing. Change your focus to one of gratitude for what you do have and what you have accomplished. Focus on your own strengths, not your weaknesses. After all, life's not a competition; it's a journey, and yours is unique to you. Give up the need to rank yourself in comparison to others.

Life's not a competition; it's a journey, and yours is unique to you.

For three days the women in my workshop share their deepest fears, their hurts and tears, and their laughter. More than anything, they demonstrate their care for one another. Eventually, instead of playing their Ego games of separation, they uncover their realness. They open their hearts and see the mirror of themselves in each other. Connected at last!

When we simply see each other as neither more nor less, we form a bond of humanity that strips away our fears. There is no hierarchy; we are all experiencing our own journeys through life. The fact is, we're more alike than different, so why play this losing game?

MY EGO SAYS

"I need to be better than you."

MY *Spirit* SAYS

"I need to be better at just being me."

11

Stuck in the Humdrum

*A*re you stuck in a humdrum routine, just getting by? Is one day limping along after the other, dragging its heels? If so, perhaps you are living in a well-worn rut of comfort and habit. It's too easy to be seduced by security and a steady lifestyle. After all, comfort doesn't call for change and it doesn't require risk. We may even rationalize that life is stressful enough without adding to the tension. Like a well-worn pair of shoes, the familiar is too easy and comfortable to

slip into. But what if life isn't about being comfortable? What if it's about growing and improving, taking risks and getting your feet dirty?

This near-life subsistence is a painful way to live and a painful way to die.

Have you ever come across people who are so dull and devoid of energy that you were tempted to put a mirror to their face to see if they were still breathing? I call them the living dead. Some are dead as early as 40 but not buried until they are 90. They go through the motions of living but in actuality are just flat-lining it. This near-life subsistence is a painful way to live and a painful way to die. Stuck in indifference and apathy, their passion withers and their Spirit slowly dies. To them, burdened by their life load, change is just another thing they have to do. It seems easier to be spectators on the sidelines of life while others join in the parade.

Perhaps you've lost your direction and need a compass to show you the way forward. Perhaps you've lost faith in yourself, choosing comfort and security over risk and the unknown. Uncertainty can play a role in keeping you stuck in a rut. When this happens, there is a tendency to settle for less and to give up before you even get started. The secret is not to let indecision bog you down, because the lure of your comfort zone may lull you into inaction.

The consistent call on my own life has been to push beyond my fears. I can now reflect on the times I showed extraordinary courage, when I stepped beyond the familiar into the unknown. I've always felt most alive after I stretched my abilities, pushed my creativity, or stepped into my fear. This feeling is often directly proportional to the discomfort I allow myself to experience.

At times, having a routine and a soft place to fall has been necessary to help me cope with life. There

have also been times when I have chosen the path of least resistance always ready with excuses, refusing to submit to a call for change. Before long, restlessness and sadness would show up, hand in hand, and urge me to pay attention to the call. And if I still didn't yield, like a disobedient child I would be sent for a time out to reflect in the silence of depression.

So if you are bored, fearful to step into the unknown, or unwilling to leave your comfort zone, know that your life is calling, and it may be time to pay attention. By not listening, you may be shortchanging yourself of a great opportunity. Stagnation and sameness are not sufficient goals for a successful life. Desperation may be the springboard to change, but why wait until you are desperate? Isn't it better to voluntarily stretch rather than be forced to do so?

You're made for much more than coasting. The truth is, a part of you yearns for a more meaningful and fulfilling life. Perhaps you even dream about the

passionate pursuit of a goal but you don't want to struggle in the process. Nobody deliberately chooses to be uncomfortable unless there's a huge payoff. More often than not, the anxiety and inconvenience are worth it. Yes, it may mean more responsibilities, but at the very least you will live an interesting life. Did you

A part of you yearns for a more meaningful and fulfilling life.

know our biggest regrets are not usually what we do but what we don't do? Life requires participation. It will move on with or without us.

A good exercise before you go to sleep at night is to ask yourself, "Did I do something today to stretch beyond my comfort zone?"

A good friend of mine got a card on his 60th birthday. On the front was the image of a magnificent sunset. Inside was the caption "See you soon ... God." Those significant birthday celebrations can be great motivators!

I encourage you to step out from the sidelines of life and join in the parade. If nothing else, the drums will keep you marching!

MY **EGO** SAYS
"I'll resist change."

MY *Spirit* SAYS
"I'll risk and allow whatever unfolds."

12

Break a Sweat Without the Workout

Menopause is a natural part of aging; like pimples and adolescence, it's just a stage. It's the end of our youth, the end of our reproductive cycles, and for most, the end of our youthful looks. But menopause is not just about endings, it's also about beginnings. Your job is to make it through the process without killing anyone!

Each aspect of menopause is unique to every woman. Some women breeze through this major life transition without even breaking their stride. How, you might ask? Maybe because they were gifted with fabulous genetics or because they allowed their hair to gray, ate organic foods, stayed close to nature, and never knew stress. I call them "nuts and berries" women. Whatever their secret is, they should bottle it and make billions. As for the rest of us, we just go nuts!

Menopause is not just about endings, it's also about beginnings.

I approached my fifties with a smug swagger. I was secure in the knowledge that I had already done "the work" necessary to heal my life. With no emotional baggage, my reward was a smooth-sailing passage through menopause, right? As they say, pride comes before a fall, and that fall was a long way down; it wasn't pretty.

Who turned up the heat? My melting moments usually occurred at the most inappropriate times. Beads of sweat would trickle down my back and dampen my brow. Later, a glimpse in a mirror would reflect a black-eyed Goth look. I'd scream in fright. "Why didn't anyone tell me my mascara had run to my chin?"

Besides my wacky internal thermometer, the hormone hell I experienced was like an unending nightmare of PMS. Like a puppeteer pulling my strings, menopause controlled my every emotion. I was irritable, moody, and depressed—usually all at the same time. I felt like an adolescent again, except without all of the raging sex hormones. They'd disappeared along with my good mood. When I'd see a Viagra advertisement with the man grinning like a Cheshire cat, I'd feel sorry for the poor woman! On a daily basis my husband would gauge whether to hide, duck, encourage, or laugh—his timing on the last one was often unfortunate. He once even dared to say, "Could you hurry up through this menopause thing? I'm not happy." Notice he only said it once!

As if heat malfunctions and crazy-making hormones weren't enough, what was happening to my brain? Have you ever found yourself halfway to somewhere—like halfway up the stairs—only to stop and wonder if you were halfway up or halfway down? Or you start a task and then notice that another needs attention, then another...only to discover, two hours of distractions later, that you still haven't completed the first task. Befuddled, unable to concentrate or focus, you're convinced you have a brain disease, especially when you can't remember squat.

Tossing and turning, blankets off, then on, then off again, restless legs, itchy skin, bladder pressure, fatigue, and a body that just won't sleep. Despite biology's whims, I think we women could manage

better if we could just get a decent night's sleep! For too many of us, what is supposed to be a natural cycle into the evening of our lives is more commonly an ordeal of feeling awful. No doubt, we're the symptom of our own lifestyles that are so far from the rhythms that nature intended. Like adolescence and its turmoil, this too will pass. It's no fun being a cantankerous old hag when you know that's not you. Take care of yourself, because one day you will emerge ready to collect your rite of passage badge—and your gift, too.

We are so far from the rhythms that nature intended.

What gift could there be in so much angst and loss? Menopause in itself is the gift. When the hormones settle and you feel more like yourself, take time for quiet introspection. There is an upside to all the downsides. When you are no longer trying to stop the clock, and when you have given up the illusion that you'll never get old, you are truly free to live your life. This is your chance to uncover any hidden desires and talents still to be expressed. It's your opportunity to connect to your inner wisdom. It's your time to reinvent and unleash creativity like you've never known before.

So despite the crumpled packaging, know your new life is waiting. Go claim your prize!

MY **EGO** SAYS
"I am my youthful good looks."

MY *Spirit* SAYS
"Ignore the packaging, the gift is inside."

13

The Sound of Silence

$\mathcal{W}$e listen to the voices of friends and loved ones telling us how to live and what to do. We are bombarded with voices from the media—television, magazines, and newspapers constantly fill our minds with visual and auditory chatter. We have been raised in a culture that fills every available space with images and sound. It's as though the din of our daily lives drowns out any chance of silence. Meanwhile our inner guidance—that calm voice of insistence

that never lets us down and never leads us astray—sits patiently in the silence waiting for us to turn down the noise.

I used to think meditation and sitting in peace was for all the "woo-woo" people. You know, the yogi types who tend to float around in pajamas and live in another reality. I didn't have time for sitting cross-legged. I didn't have time to spend hours chanting. I was busy and preoccupied with creating my life. I was charging forward, head bent into the wind, feet planted firmly on the ground, and a heart controlled by my commands. Anything else was drifting out there, so heavenly bound it was no earthly good. Boy, was I wrong!

So what changed my mind? My inner voice did an amazing sales job! I started to notice that when I did listen to my inner voice, great things happened. Like the time I was prompted to call on my neighbor Joanne. I didn't really know her beyond the pleasantries we shared over the fence and I felt uncomfortable just inviting myself over. At first I tried to ignore the inner voice and rationalized that it was just a silly notion, but it persisted. I grabbed some lilacs from my garden and gave her door a rap. Tearfully, she shared that she'd just been diagnosed with breast cancer and was terrified.

A friendship was built that day that not only gave her the encouragement and support she needed but also gave me the confidence to listen to that inner voice. If I had been caught up in the dizzy pace of life, I wouldn't have heard, or perhaps wouldn't have taken action on, what my inner voice was trying to tell me. On numerous occasions I have been led to close encounters of the real kind, with outcomes that made me shake my head in disbelief.

Our inner guidance sits in the silence waiting for us to turn down the noise.

Do I now float around in loose pants and rebuke those people still stuck in the rat race? Heck no! I still

look normal on the outside, but there's been a radical shift inside. For starters, life is no longer a race. Whew!

Today I allow my life to happen with faith and trust instead of forcing it with fear and control. When I become distracted and allow myself to get seduced back into the racket and clamor of life, I notice how quickly I lose my balance. I become too easily stressed or ignore someone who needs a minute of my time. And when I'm off balance, I often lose my way. My busy thoughts overtake the quieter pace of living that calls out from my heart. Then once again, yearning to make meaning of the madness, I rediscover that quiet inner chamber where my true guidance resides, and I wonder why I ever left.

I have a chaise by the window in my bedroom. This is my sanctuary. I escape to it often. It is here that I have learned to silence my thoughts and sit in the stillness that follows. This is where creative ideas blossom, where troubles get sorted, and where peace is there for the

asking. It took time for me to recognize the voice inside.
I call it the voice of Spirit. It never shouts or preaches.
Instead, it guides and gently suggests what I need to
know. Sometimes I get directed to do things I really
hadn't thought of or don't really want to do. I have come
to trust this inner wisdom.

MY EGO SAYS
*"Listen to me and
do it my way."*

MY *Spirit* SAYS
*"Wisdom is in
the silence,
if you'll listen."*

14

Bernadette

$\mathcal{I}$ find it baffling how children can grow up in the
same home and recall conflicting experiences. For
a long time it was difficult for me to remember the
fun and happy childhood times—birthday parties
and family holidays. They were buried under painful
memories that dominated and obscured everything
else. Those early years were painted with a heavy
coat of hurt and fear. Interestingly, my five siblings
often had different stories of childhood and I often

questioned my own sanity. Did we even live in the same house?

Reminiscing with my siblings over the years has been a bittersweet experience. My family has helped me remember carefree times and challenged my childhood echo of pain and anxiety with the lighter memories of growing up. However, the surfacing of the pleasant memories also brought up experiences that I had buried deep inside the archives of my childhood, memories of shame and remorse.

Her name was Bernadette and she came from a family of thirteen children. She was dirt poor, her poverty hanging in rags on her thin frame. Bernadette wore plastic sandals no matter what the weather, with no socks to keep her feet warm. Nobody wanted to be her friend. She was too different and too dirty. Unkempt, unwashed, and all alone, she was an easy target for bullies like me. There was a hierarchy in the school; there were the favored kids and then there

were the rest of us. When it came to the pecking order however, Bernadette was even lower and more vulnerable than I was.

Recess was a time I dreaded. Outside, in the concrete yard within the confines of the high brick walls, the playground felt more like a jail to me. I didn't want to run around with the others. They seemed free and happy to play, but I just felt trapped. I wasn't alone.

Everyone experiences regret and remorse at some time in their lives.

Across the schoolyard, Bernadette skulked in a corner, defeated and ignored like a bad smell. I saw my opportunity. I started to stalk her in the playground. I enrolled another girl as an accomplice; taunting and teasing her became a game. Bernadette ran away to avoid our bullying, but like a pack of rabid dogs we were on to her. My sidekick and I followed her into the bathroom—her preferred hiding place—and peeked under the stall. I was a six-year-old bully and my aim was to make her life more miserable than mine. As I type this story and remember back half a century ago, my eyes fill with tears for Bernadette and sadness for the six-year-old child I was then. I still feel remorse for what I did.

Everyone experiences regret and remorse at some time in their lives. Whether it's words we've said and wished to take back, or something we've done or failed to do. The fact that we remember these incidents and feel remorse means we have already begun to learn from them. It's better late than never.

The reminders and the remorse are not there to hold us hostage but to heal our hearts if we choose to do so. It's not helpful to condemn ourselves, wallow in regret, or try wriggling off the hook. We must face things head on without deception, excuses, or illusions, or resign ourselves to living a life of "If only" and "I wish." There are steps you can take to help the healing process:

- Acknowledge what you've done, and make amends if you can.

- If you feel remorse, it can be revealing to relive the incident.

- Put yourself back in your own shoes and recall the circumstances. What was going on at the time? What did you need that you were not getting? It might be that this was the best you could do under the particular circumstances.

- If you feel anger, you need to express it. Write in a journal, talk to someone, or punch a pillow—whatever works.

- Finally, find compassion and forgive yourself.

From my bittersweet memoirs I close this chapter from my childhood.

Bernadette and I meet for coffee. It is a wonderful cozy café, a far cry from the cold brick walls and concrete playground. She has risen far above her difficult circumstances. I'm delighted to hear that she's doing well. Bernadette reaches across the table, takes my hands in hers, and says that she forgives me. And that's when I wake up.

Bernadette, I may never get the opportunity to meet you face to face again, but wherever you are, my heart says, "I'm sorry."

MY **EGO** SAYS

"I'm not guilty, why should I feel remorse?"

MY *Spirit* SAYS

"I was wrong. I'm sorry."

15

Sticks and Stones

I think stupid became part of my DNA from the early age of seven; I certainly heard it often enough. My elementary school teachers were especially venomous. Not knowing the answer to a question would earn me a knuckle thump to the head, followed by "Stupid!" My father picked up on the name-calling where my teachers left off. If the teachers thought I was stupid, I must have been. He wasn't about to argue with them. The damage to my

self-concept took years to undo.

I have worked hard to uncover and eliminate many of those labels. The ones that stuck the most were the ones that came loaded with an emotional punch—*stupid*, *dummy*, and *liar*. The pain I experienced at the time, and the virulence of those words repeated over and over again, set those labels in concrete. I was tired of dragging them around like heavy blocks tied to my ankles.

Sticks and stones may break our bones but names *do* hurt.

When parents, teachers, or other authority figures label children judgmentally, negatively, or harshly, the words tend to stick. Words have indelible power over us, especially when they are constantly repeated.

But it's not only adults who carelessly lash out with their tongues. Children as young as five regularly participate in harassing and name-calling. If a child is different in any way, he or she is a target for teasing.

Weirdo, geek, dummy, fatso—these labels can play a powerful role in a child's development and even become part of his or her identity. Parents today are fearful of guns and knives in their children's schools, but taunting and verbal harassment are weapons that can be just as damaging.

Brothers and sisters can also be guilty of taunting and teasing. Parents tend to ignore this or treat it as a normal part of family life. The perpetrator gets away with it by saying "I was only joking," and parents continue to turn a deaf ear.

But isn't teasing a part of growing up? Unfortunately yes, but what is natural or normal about wanting to hurt someone with a derogatory name or label?

Look back into your own life experience. Do you remember being called names or labeled in any way? You might be amazed at what you'll remember. Labels can be imposed from the outside by others or from the inside by your own self-talk. You may have

continued the name-calling where others left off by internally beating yourself up. Even well-meaning parents label their children with seemingly innocuous labels: "She's the athletic one" or "He's the clever one." However, these labels can unwittingly burden children with expectations. They can change them at the core of who they are and push them to become what the label tells them to be.

Sticks and stones may break our bones, but names do hurt.

Did the labels—the negative or the seemingly positive ones—change who you are? Are you tired of dragging them around as if they belong to you?

A ceremonial way to free yourself from labels is to find a stick or a stone and let it represent a name or a label you want to let go of. If you can remember a particularly painful event relating to this label, all the better. Grab the stick or stone, and with power and conviction say, "I refuse to carry you around anymore"—or something less polite. But say it like you mean it. Chuck the object as far away as you can. If you feel emotional, let the feelings come; cry, scream, get mad, do whatever you need to do to let the emotions go. You'll feel a lot lighter for it.

This is the Irish version of the famous rhyme:

Sticks and stones may break my bones,
But names will never hurt me.
And when I'm dead and in my grave,
You'll suffer what you'd called me.

We Irish like to add an extra burden of guilt to our nursery rhymes!

MY **EGO** SAYS
"I'm as stupid as
they say I am."

MY *Spirit* SAYS
"I'm not defined by
what they say."

16

When the Sizzle has Fizzled

$\mathcal{D}$uring my late teens and early twenties my hormones were at their peak. Of course, biology deliberately plans it that way to keep the planet procreating. Unaware of nature's bigger purpose, I was hot and I knew it! From the provocative way I dressed to the confident way I walked into a room, my image screamed desirable, delicious, and sexy. In my youthful naivety, I was looking for love. In reality, I was serving myself up on a platter as fertile fodder!

Now, as I look back, my heart aches for my younger self. I'm also envious of the vibrant sexual essence that was so bountiful in my youth.

Early in my marriage, when our children were little, my sexual energy waned. I would often blame exhaustion. I was horrified to discover later that part of my sexual lassitude was a consequence of treating my husband as one of the children! Nurturing a family can be an all-inclusive and all-encompassing endeavor, and it was easier for me to include him in my maternal bubble. I was so consumed with playing the nurturing mother that I set aside and shelved the sensuous wife.

Because of my own experience, I have often counseled young women to be aware of this lure of motherhood and to instead stay committed to their primary intimate relationship. "Keep your date nights; keep the romance alive; and don't mother your husband," I'd caution. Of course, as a young mother this is easier said than done.

It is difficult to be intimate and somehow pull sexy out of a hat when all you really want is to collapse into bed cocooned in your favorite flannels and sleep for a year! With your changed body image, hormone swings, and the stress of new responsibilities, you may even question and doubt your relationship. "Why don't I find myself sexually attracted to him anymore?" Just because your sex drive is different doesn't always mean there's something amiss with your relationship.

Despite the demands of motherhood, stay committed to your primary intimate relationship.

From my research, losing your mojo and occasionally experiencing a lackluster sex life seems to be a fairly common occurrence. No matter what stage we are at in life, I think it's very dangerous for us to assume a relationship malfunction when we lose sexual interest. It may be that you're "just not into him" for a while. As long as there is an emotional and spiritual connection, relationships can usually withstand the occasional sexual drought.

For some relationships, a lessened sex drive isn't a big issue and is often replaced by other intimate and bonding experiences. However, if sex is important to either partner and is ignored for too long, the unmet expectations and building frustration can lead to feelings of resentment, rejection, and damaged Egos. If one or both of you are struggling, and you can't seem to resolve it on your own, get some advice from experienced professionals who can help. Because when the sizzle has fizzled it's not only the physical connection that suffers; the emotional and spiritual bonds that are vital to an intimate relationship can be lost as well.

Which brings me again to peri-menopause and menopause. Okay, so your biology is now saying, "It's over—no more babies." In case you needed any more proof, your breasts and buttocks head south, your

libido sags, and your hail-damaged thighs won't look sexy no matter what you wear—or don't wear. Great! How unfair is that? And that's not all. Just as he stocks up on Viagra, wacky hormones confuse your mind into thinking that your partner who used to be a hunk is now looking much too old to play with!

I know hormones get a bad rap and are not always the cause of a low sex drive, but if you suspect they might be a problem, get yourself checked. Having low testosterone levels is linked to experiencing a low libido. Considering the stresses we contend with and the polluted environment we live in, it's virtually impossible not to encounter hormone imbalance at some stage of our lives.

Dr. Phil often counsels, "If you have a good sex life, it is ten percent of the relationship; but if you don't, it is ninety percent." Be proactive and pay attention to this prediction. And if a lower libido isn't bothering you, your partner, or your relationship, then take heart—perhaps nature has had the last word after all.

^{MY} **EGO** _{SAYS}

"I don't feel like having sex; it must be your fault."

^{MY} *Spirit* _{SAYS}

"I don't feel like having sex, but I still love you."

17

The Ego's Stance

I believe that my need to be right is a consequence of a childhood where I often felt wrong. The authority figures in my life had all the power and I was told they were always right. I was reminded daily that I was powerless; I felt angry and afraid. As I grew up, I wanted that control—I wanted to be the one who was right. So I learned to fight, shout, and stand my ground rather than ever feel bullied and threatened again.

I have had several heated arguments with my husband over the years. My voice was the loudest—as if being louder would win. No matter how compelling his argument was, I wouldn't or couldn't fold. I would use my memory and intellect to drive home my point. For what? My weary, worn-down husband would eventually say, "You're right." I would win, only later to feel I'd lost.

There really is nothing wrong with being right, however, it's the need to be right all the time that can be deadly.

If I am always right, then what does that make you? Always wrong! How endearing is that? This mental dynamic perpetuates separation and conflict in our relationships. And who is the culprit? Ego.

When we assert our will over others, it is Ego that is playing us. Like an imposter, it takes over our minds and our mouths. Whenever we feel threatened in a me-versus-you situation, it's Ego that armors up and goes to war. When we must have the last word to prove how right we are, it's our threatened Ego needing to mark its territory. Afraid of losing, it will do whatever it needs to stay protected; it promotes this high drama to assert its authority. Ego is all about me; there's no you in it. On the surface this may appear as a win-lose situation in relationships. I win, you lose. But at a deeper level it's really lose-lose; nobody wins.

When we assert our will over others, it is Ego that is playing us.

Learning how to get out of your head and into your heart is essential for curbing the power of your Ego. It makes a huge difference when you reset your dial from headstrong and rigid to empathy and understanding.

It's also important to recognize how often your Ego tries to gain control.

A trigger for me is any time I feel threatened or afraid of being wrong. In the past I would cling to my

Ego like a life raft, only to discover too late it was steering me toward the rapids. Now I'm aware when my voice gets shrill—it goes up at least three decibels! I feel like something is at war inside, so I need to stop and breathe. I ask myself, "Who is talking here?" If it's my Ego, I consciously separate myself from the feelings that I'm experiencing. Instead of reacting, I observe and detach myself from my Ego's need to trample on someone else's point of view. Only through this awareness can I see the other person, hear what he or she is saying, and transcend my Ego. This takes continuous practice.

When you surrender your agenda to be right, you have the opportunity to listen to another person's perspective. By doing so, you get to understand the other position fully before you present your own. You may not agree, but see if you can remain open and accept that there are differences. The interaction then becomes about me and you, and there's still a connection in the relationship. On occasion there may be situations where you are absolutely right. The question is, can you feel content knowing you are right without making the other person wrong?

If what I think is true and what I think is false are matters of perception, then I need to be wary. What if my views are distorted? This is a humbling truth. My problem is, I speak with such passion and conviction that I sell myself on my own words. I am learning to pay attention and to embrace other perspectives and differences rather than create polarity and disconnection.

Remain open and accept there will be differences.

As a couple, my husband and I identify when either of us falls into this need-to-be-right trap. We've discovered that using humor is a great diffuser of tension. However, like any great comedian knows, the timing and tone are critical. I'd tease and say, "You're right; I agree that you're better than me." The quizzical look on my husband's face would have us laughing in no time.

MY **EGO** SAYS
*"I'm right and I
don't care what
you think or feel."*

MY *Spirit* SAYS
*"I have an opinion,
but I'm open to listening."*

18

Fumbling Forward

I love those books where the heroine bravely packs up her old life and steps into the unknown. I live my life precariously through her adventures. I cheer her on as she fumbles forward, risking it all. Of course, reading books is the safest way to explore.

What if you knew that you could not fail? Like living a story with a happy ending? That no matter what you risked in your life today, success was guaranteed?

With this assurance, no longer restrained by the fear of the unknown, your world would suddenly become alive with activity. You'd be striving and thriving with anticipation and expectation.

Why are we so afraid to risk making a mistake? Perhaps it's because we've been programmed to see failure and errors as a bad thing. But isn't it true that mistakes are mistakes only if we don't learn from them? An "oops" in your life can be incredibly beneficial. I agree, it isn't the nicest feeling when you've realized you've tripped up, but at least make that blunder worthwhile by learning from it.

If we don't risk making a mistake, we may risk losing even more.

Everyone makes mistakes. It's part of being human. How can we become wise if we never make a mistake? How will we ever know what is possible if we don't explore outside our comfort zone? If we don't risk making a mistake, we may risk losing even more.

I'm reminded of the time when I was ready for a new career. At the time I was stuck doing office work at my husband's

Follow what your Spirit says instead of listening to your perfectionist Ego.

business. Day in and day out I'd drag myself to work, unhappy and unchallenged, bored with the dull routine. I had known for a long time that I needed a change, but the fear of making a mistake stopped me in my tracks. I wanted desperately to push beyond the four walls of the office and explore new territories such as teaching and writing, but I was constantly restrained by a backdraft of fear.

Despite the possibility of expanding my capacity, my protectionist Ego would wrap me tightly, secure in the roots of the familiar. "Don't be foolish. You're not qualified for anything else. Besides, it's not such a bad job, and the hours are good." So I'd remain immobile and even rationalize my decision to stay stuck; I justified how leaving was not an option because I would be letting my husband down. He needed me because the company was in a critical stage of growth. I felt hopeless, I was miserable and I wanted out.

What if I make a wrong decision? What if I regret my choice? Should I wait? Uncertainty and fear kept me petrified and frozen for over a year. Then one day I hit bottom—my day of desperation, when the frustration of my inaction became more painful than my fears. I made the decision to leave. I was finally willing to take a leap of faith and risk falling on my face, but that was preferable to dying inside. Anaïs Nin said it beautifully: "And the day came when the risk to remain tight in a bud was more painful than the risk it took to blossom." I left the office routine to pursue my creative talents, and I've never looked back.

Everyone faces the fear of stepping out of a comfort zone. The key is to keep moving, learning, and growing, accepting that fear is a natural part of the journey of life.

I've discovered that moving from a state of inertia is more difficult than when I have some momentum. It's like riding my bicycle up a hill. If I stop halfway, it is more difficult to get going again than if I'd just kept slowly cycling upward. Instead of quitting, I could have kept pedaling with my eyes focused on the crest of the hill.

Now, I trip up, mess up, and screw up consistently. My children believe it's old age setting in, but I call it growth. Sometimes my slip-ups knock me back in the confidence department. I may falter for a while, but I always bounce back. I prefer to make choices, following what my Spirit says instead of listening to my perfectionist Ego. Although I still need courage to step up and step out, I've noticed that fear is diminished in the light of my Spirit. I trust that if I fall, there's a valid reason for it.

When faced with an important decision, a great question to ask is, "What's the worst that could happen?" If your answer is a bruised Ego, is it still worth it? I don't know about you, but I'd rather lose face and be rejected than go to my grave with the regret of not having lived fully.

MY **EGO** SAYS

"I will just die if I fail."

MY *Spirit* SAYS

"Everyone dies but not everyone really lives."

19

Confession

When I was growing up, my devout mother would insist that it was necessary to confess my sins to the priest. A typical disclosure would be, "I hit my sister," or "I told my mummy a lie," or "I stole a biscuit from the tin." I remember on occasion making up stories as I didn't want to sound too repetitive week after week. After all, I didn't want to waste the priest's time. As a child, confessing my misdeeds was just a routine, although I must admit the fears of having to confess

did somewhat temper my naughty ways. Recently, in an entirely different setting, I finally understood the healing power of confession.

Memories of childhood came flooding back as I grieved the loss of my father. I remembered our happy times together, the family adventures we had, traveling together and camping like gypsies. Then there were the not-so-great times of angry voices and feeling afraid. As I remembered the happy and the sad times, painful emotions sat heavily on my heart, and I just couldn't shake them. I concluded that the emotional burden I felt was the lingering sadness and pain of my father's death. I believed time would eventually take care of the heaviness.

I threw myself back into life, all the while feeling like I was dragging around a wagonload of grief. Time passed. Then more time, and still the oppressive emotions sat stubborn and unmoving, crowding out my freedom and joy. As a teacher and a facilitator of

healing, I was used to holding the mirror for others. I knew it was time to practice what I preached. It was time to stop being distracted by life and to grieve properly. It was time to let go and feel what I needed to feel. Little did I know what was about to be purged.

I set aside a whole day to grieve. Within the confines of my bedroom I set up a slide show of my dad. I put on the saddest music I could find, made sure the tissues were handy and allowed the tears to flow. Then, shortly after I'd started crying, the tears just stopped. I was shocked. That's it? Is this all the love I had for my dad? Was I such a cold and unfeeling daughter? Or had I already done my grieving during his illness these past few years? I sat and waited.

Then, like an unplugged volcano, it erupted. Like molten lava, all the unexpressed anger and hurt that had been locked in my cells for a lifetime spewed out. A torrent of red-hot anger replaced the gray heaviness of grief; it was anger that had clogged my energy and blocked my heart. Out it came—the injustices of childhood, the pain of not feeling loved. I shouted, I yelled, and I screamed with abandon. There was no way I could stop the barrage; it had been stuffed inside for so long. Layer upon layer it erupted; the release was painful.

Healing grief is impossible without first releasing anger. Healing needs to start from the top down, and anger is always the first layer.

By attempting to grieve first, I had unwittingly attempted to heal backwards. I would never have been able to reach the pain and sorrow of my loss without dealing with the anger first.

My father wasn't the only recipient of my anger. Everyone who had ever betrayed me triggered more ranting. I was center stage too; the virulence of the anger of self-reproach shocked me. I was ashamed of my lack of empathy for my father, for permitting the stuff of life to constrain my compassion and limit the time I spent with him. My Ego had pointed the finger, condemning him again and again, and my hardened heart had listened. I sobbed until there were no more tears left, and then silence

There is healing power in confession.

filled the space. New emotions surfaced, the familiar ones of guilt and remorse.

I yearned for contrition—anything to appease these heavy feelings. Just as I had done so many years before, I started my confession. My tears said, "I'm sorry, forgive me." This time I didn't need to make up anything. I had plenty of sins to unload. I asked my dad to forgive me and slowly I surrendered the guilt, remorse, and regrets—anything that had prevented my heart from loving him fully. I felt his forgiveness. Like balm on an open wound, peace soothed my aching heart and healed my broken Spirit. I was able to forgive

my father, and with compassion for my humanness,
I was then able to forgive myself.

MY EGO SAYS
*"I don't need to
be forgiven."*

MY *Spirit* SAYS
"Forgive me."

20

The Quitting Habit

*H*ave you ever undertaken something only to discover you lose steam and have difficulty following through? Take mastering a new habit. For example, you decide it's time to get fit. You set up an exercise schedule to get your body in shape and you're excited as you visualize a healthier, toned, glowing you. You've gone shopping and bought the latest fancy runners and a pair of super-sucking spandex shorts. You are pumped and committed! After the first week

of rising early for some weightlifting and a jog you are feeling great. "Not too bad," you think. "I can do this!"

However, by week three the weather is decidedly cooler; plus you had to skip your schedule twice already to attend to more important things. By week five it's definitely harder to stay enthused; after all, you had expected to look like an Olympian goddess by now and it's obvious that those super-sucking spandex shorts are still doing most of the toning. By the first signs of frost on the road you have cooled to the whole idea, making excuses to go for it in the spring instead.

Once the initial rush for the desired goal has fizzled out, the inconvenience and discomfort of your new reality sets in. Beware! Or should I say, "Be aware."

What do you say to yourself when things get tough? Is your mental switch automatically set on "quit"? Internal messages can literally take you out of the race at the first hurdle. What if we'd decided as toddlers

that standing up and falling down a hundred times a day was just too much work and learning to walk just wasn't worth the effort? How ridiculous would that be?

When your willpower ebbs and flows like a tide, you won't succeed. When you quit part way and never finish what you start, you won't succeed. If you don't have the discipline when the going gets tough, you

What do you say to yourself when things get tough?

definitely won't succeed. However, when you have a strong will, combined with persistence and self-discipline, nothing can stop you.

Life today is all about the speed at which we can get things done. Our instant-gratification genes are offended if we have to wait for anything. We Google something and the wait time for a download is two minutes; no way, we're already off surfing somewhere else. The sales person at the store is moving at a snail's pace and we're ready to kill. Cook a meal from scratch? But we're hungry now, so we grab a microwave dinner from the freezer. Just put us in a queue at the bank, or worse, tell us to please hold for the next available representative—it's not always a pretty sight!

Many children have also been raised to expect immediate results and they often feel entitled to be given what they want rather than having to wait. The concept of expecting them to hold off until a birthday for a new toy, or to save their allowance to buy a new computer game, is becoming as extinct as the dinosaurs.

The truth is, we want the fastest, most comfortable, least resistant way to accomplish our goals. Or, like a petulant child, we quit in a tantrum. If new disciplines require work and effort, and new habits take time and commitment, what the heck are we going to do about this conundrum? How will we ever know the thrill of climbing a mountain or enjoy the satisfaction of learning a new language? Is "no pain, no gain" just a nonsensical quote?

When someone tells me, "You're very impatient," I know it's true. I am my father's daughter. Even though I witnessed this trait in my dad and thought it most unbecoming, I wrestle with it too. If there's a dawdler holding up traffic, I'm not the one sending good vibes. If someone in the fast-food line is having trouble choosing what to order, I come close to losing it. I accomplish many tasks at the speed of light and consequently experience the highs of immediate fulfillment. This momentum is invigorating, but the downside is that I'm focused only on short-term successes. Long-term goals require perseverance and a commitment to delayed gratification. For me that's something new and not always easy. But it's working. Believe me, if I can persist, resist, and see it through without quitting or killing the slowpokes, anyone can!

If you've struggled with this, recognize the challenge and change your attitude to one of "I am going to see this through no matter what!" This is an intractable and committed mindset. Adopt a no-exceptions policy. When you are tired and just don't feel like exercising, do you quit? No! When you have self-doubt and are very tempted to make an excuse as to why it won't work, do you quit? No! When someone tells you to cut yourself some slack and cheat a little on your diet, do you listen? No!

Adopt a no-exceptions policy.

Instead, keep your eyes focused on your goal and envision how great it will be to accomplish it—see it through.

MY **EGO** SAYS
"I'll quit if it isn't easy."

MY *Spirit* SAYS
"I'll persevere until I make it."

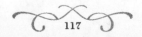

21

What I Wish I'd Known

*T*errified, I clung onto the tiny handhold on the climbing wall. I dared not look down, I was already sick with dizziness. The fear in my chest squeezed my heart like a drum; each beat—dadum, dadum, dadum—reminded me, "You can do this." Sure I can do it—if the fright of it doesn't kill me first!

It's been said that what doesn't kill us will make us stronger. If that's true, I must be Hercules by now.

Life has certainly been a test.
Having stumbled my way to
maturity, I now realize the
measure of wisdom I have
gleaned from living life. Oh,

*What doesn't kill us
will make us stronger.*

how I could have used that awareness, clarity and
experience when I was much younger.

What if you were able to speak to your younger self?
What do you know now about life that you wish you
had known then?

I'd say something like this:

Dear Little Curly Head:
You are only nine years old and already you're
afraid of life. I feel sad for you as I remember
the confusion and anxiety you are feeling. Your
sensitive nature is a little trodden right now,
but your stubborn streak is simmering too and
this will keep your Spirit alive. I know your
teachers are bullies and going to school is a

nightmare. I wish Mum and Dad were open to listening or that I could be there to defend you and turn the cane on them. I know you have been taught to respect people in authority but some people don't deserve your respect or your trust. I know right now you believe you're a dunce. Little one, what if I told you instead that you are smart, bright, and creative? Adults are not always right and your teachers are really dragons in disguise. Right now you need a feast of love and encouragement; instead you'll get by on the crumbs of your own courage.

Take hope in the fact that these painful experiences are not wasted, because in the future they will be used in a very positive way to help others. In fact, your own children will never suffer oppression at school like you did. Why? Because your eagle eyes will be on constant watch, guarding their tender psyches.

You're a sensitive child; you make things harder in your own mind. Your feelings run deep and you want to make everyone happy. I know you want to please Mum and Dad but you often feel like a disappointment to them. They are doing their best, just coping with life and managing a house full of children. Dear Little One: you are not alone in your angst and shame. God is not the bogeyman in the sky, and Mum will not sell you to the gypsies. In fact, there are lots of fun and exciting times ahead.

I know you don't believe it but Mum and Dad really do love you and show it as best they can. Little One, the way you see your life right now is distorted. It's like looking at yourself in those crazy mirrors at a carnival. Later in life you will get the chance to rearrange this reflection and find your awesome true self.

Don't worry about being picked last for a team. Not everyone will understand or appreciate who you are and what you have to offer. You must learn not to internalize their rejection. I know this is difficult to do. Remember, it's not always about you. Learn how to champion yourself and become your own encourager.

Don't try so hard to be liked and to fit in; it only diminishes you. It really doesn't matter what other people think. It's better to be yourself in all things. I know you don't think much of yourself right now, but that will change. Stop comparing yourself to others around you. Remember, there will always be girls that are smarter, prettier, and richer than you are and then there'll be girls who are not. I can't believe Mum let your hair grow into an Afro—definitely not your best look! However, you will grow into a beautiful young woman and get more than enough of the attention you crave, some of it the wrong kind. But that's another chapter.

Life is not always fair, and I wish I could tell you it's all going to work out soon. You have many rocky patches ahead, adolescence being one of them. Laugh, have fun, and stop fighting with your siblings. I know you don't care for them now but you'll grow to love them all. Take faith in the fact that eventually you will come to cherish them.

MY EGO SAYS

"I was always the least."

MY *Spirit* SAYS

*"You are more because
you were less."*

22

Resentment—a Recipe for War

My husband gets the silent treatment when he ignores how I feel about something. If I am feeling upset and he changes the subject, this will clamp my mouth shut tighter than a clam. As my resentment stews, I clatter the pots loudly in the kitchen just to make sure he knows he's in trouble. My passionate performance could win an Oscar for best actress in a silent movie. It usually doesn't take him long to come around, especially at meal times, because he

likes to eat and I'm the cook!

What causes me to act like this? Resentment—that little pissed-off feeling you get when someone ignores your needs, steps over your boundaries, or demands too much. Milder than the heat of anger, but simmering with enough steam to hurt yourself and those you care about most, resentment can negatively affect everyone in its path.

> *When resentment takes hold in a relationship, it can build for years.*

We get resentful when our needs or expectations are not being met. Perhaps one person doesn't get enough support from his or her partner or feels there's a lack of communication. The other person in the relationship may not think the issue is a big deal and ignores the partner. Whatever the problem, whether real or perceived, can lead to resentment if not addressed. When resentment takes hold in a relationship, it can build for years. It blocks connection and intimacy, undermines trust, and corrodes healthy communication. The aftermath is a vicious cycle of negativity that chips away at the wounded relationship. Over time these unmet needs stack up like dirty laundry. They may be tossed aside but they're not forgotten. Resentment can have a really long memory.

It's very rare to have only one person in a relationship carrying all the resentment; both parties are usually sucked in. My mentor, George Addair, explains it best. George says there are three stages in the resentment process. First we get the feeling of resentment and, if it is not resolved, we move to second base and become resistant—there's no way we're going to cooperate! Then revenge, the "get-back" part, kicks in. If one person in a partnership feels the resentment, resistance, and revenge of the other, they too can get caught up in the same cycle.

Let's look at a hypothetical situation. Helen is resentful that Don isn't contributing to the family income. This has been an ongoing issue since Don was laid off two years ago. Helen feels he ignores the problem, and that enrages her even more. Helen wants to talk to Don in a reasonable way, but often her resentment results in a shouting match instead.

Don is resentful too. Helen uses her credit card to buy extras that she claims are necessary, but Don knows they're luxuries. He claims he feels like a bad child. He knows he needs to find a job, but when Helen keeps bringing it up he gets defensive. Instead of communicating, he decompresses by hiding in the den with a few beers. He knows there's no point trying to make up in bed; Helen just turns her back and pretends to be asleep. Don defiantly meets with his friends at lunch when he knows he should be job searching. The waitress at the restaurant likes to chat him up, and that makes him feel good. He resents Helen and just wishes they could start over with a clean slate.

This scenario of resentment is played out in relationships around the world. The details may be different but the patterns are the same. Resentment can become so ingrained in a partnership that neither party can pinpoint what exactly is wrong with their dysfunctional relationship. The issues come spewing out only

Don't let your resentment stew. Nip it in the bud.

when the relationship is on the brink of ending. Counseling offices and divorce courts are filled with the fallout of unresolved resentment.

Other couples who stay in the dysfunctional relationship, choose to numb out instead. Tired of all the games, they repress their feelings in order to sustain a minimal level of comfort. However, repressed feelings do not disappear. Tucked away in the subconscious, they can take on a life of their own, creating anxiety, dysfunctional behavior, lethargy, illness, and disease.

Don't let your resentment stew. Nip it in the bud. As with anything that needs maintenance, monitor your relationship often and take quality time alone together where you can have meaningful communication.

Whenever I resented my husband, I always expected that he'd be the one to suffer the most. But, like bad karma, I noticed I was the one suffering. It was only me lying awake at night with a stomachache or migraine. I still bang the pans around on occasion, but it doesn't last long. My Ego likes to put on a show, but I know it's better to talk than to suppress; besides, sleep wins over revenge.

MY **EGO** SAYS
"You should know how I feel."

MY *Spirit* SAYS
"We need to talk."

23

"Thank You"—More Than Manners

$\mathcal{A}$s children, we are taught to say thank you. It's the expected polite response, and because we want to please our parents we play along. However, like a childhood rhyme memorized by heart, too often our thank you becomes rote and said without much sincerity. On occasion, when we're truly grateful, we say thank you and actually mean it.

Why do we find it difficult to be thankful? Part of the problem is we take things for granted. With a sense of entitlement and an egotistic mindset, we are blinded to the life-enriching habit of being thankful. It's like the drone of our discontent deafens the beat of our hearts. The Ego keeps us unconscious. When the shutters are closed, the sunlight simply cannot get through.

Gratitude comes from your Spirit. Unimpeded, it fills your heart and the words "thank you" fall effortlessly from your lips. Like a wave of grace, gratitude ripples far beyond your sight and returns to you again and again. A grateful heart combined with love will expand and bring you even more to be grateful for. When you live life with an attitude of gratitude, your eyes are opened to see the joy in everyday situations. With a thankful heart you cannot help but experience the happiness and hope in life, because this is living from your Spirit.

When I was diagnosed with cancer at age 33, I was terrified. I believed the doctor when he said I was going to die. I had many anguished, dark nights of the soul. I begged, bargained, and pleaded for my healthy life back. If you had told me then to find gratitude in my heart, I would have knocked your lights out! It was only later, when I had survived my illness, that I realized the incredible gifts I'd been given during that time of adversity and suffering. That illness woke me up and saved

Gratitude ripples far beyond your sight and returns to you again and again.

my life. I now appreciate each and every day. Thank you, thank you, thank you! It's easy to be thankful when we're happy and enjoying the celebrations of life. But what do you do when your heart is closed and life is tough?

Choosing to be grateful on a daily basis, no matter what life throws your way, is a tall order. But that decision can undeniably change your life for the better; there is healing power in gratitude. Once you have surrendered to this ideal, life will conspire to keep you grateful. Consequently, you receive more and more to be thankful for. It may take time and effort to make this an unconscious habit. You may even need to remind yourself daily to say, "For this too I give thanks." Persist, and a day will come when you'll notice your heart is so full that you just have to share it or burst.

If I go to bed grumpy at the end of a long, hard day, my husband, like my conscience, will not let me sleep. He'll nudge me and say, "Five things you're grateful for today." I turn my back and tell him to be quiet. He'll nudge me again—now he's really starting to bug me! "Five things you're grateful for." After more than 30 years with this man, I know how irritatingly persistent he can be. He'll even risk wrath and bodily injury to get what he wants. "Five things ..." I know I'll never get to sleep. Grudgingly, I give in, "I am grateful for this bed that I can *sometimes* get to sleep in." "I am grateful for the phone call today from my sister ..." By the time I get to five, my resistance is gone and my heart has softened.

Thank you. These simple unassuming words contain the power to change your life for the better. Say them often and with sincerity.

MY EGO SAYS
"Show me happiness and I will be grateful."

MY *Spirit* SAYS
"I am grateful, therefore I am happy."

24

Aging Without the Angst

*I*s getting older all about disintegration? If so, it's little wonder we look toward aging with a sense of dread. For most of us, this is a deeply rooted belief. If we take to heart all the messages bombarding us today, getting old is just not acceptable. No doubt with age we experience a gradual change in our outward appearance and the possibility of failing health. So how could people be happy as they age? Yet when questioned, many older women claim that

they have never felt happier and are quite adamant that they don't feel old.

I have observed that women in all age groups will willingly dole out a king's ransom to hang onto their youthful looks. Whether they are as young as 20 or as mature as 70, they will carve, starve, tuck, and suck their sagging parts to prevent and delay this dreaded impending disintegration.

I look in the mirror and ask, "Who the heck are you?" I feel like the same person inside, but someone has altered my face. As I age, I know the healthiest thing I can do is to accept the process. Naturally, I do what I can to gracefully let go and reconcile myself to the inevitable. When I notice that my conversations are too frequently about health issues, I consciously change the topic. Why add ammunition to the belief that it's all downhill from here? I tell my friends, "If I ever start talking about my bowel movements, just shoot me!"

Now that I am in my fifties, I've noticed I can walk into a mall and feel invisible. This is a new revelation to me and it was shocking at first. When did that happen? I am now camouflaged among the many monochromatic middle-aged shoppers, incognito and flying under the radar. I do feel a certain freedom and power in my new subterfuge. Nobody notices or cares that I have traded in my high heels for a comfortable pair of flats. However, there are times that I also feel discarded and ignored. It's as though I've disappeared. Do I really believe that unless I am noticed I am dispensable? I hope not.

From my earliest memories I can hear myself shout, "Look at me. Look at what I can do!" Like any child, I wanted attention, and being one of six children made this especially difficult. In fact, to get any special attention when I was younger was exhausting! As I grew up, the "notice me" became about the fashions

I wore, the sexuality I exuded, and the dramas I created. All played out on the stage called life.

So what happens as we age and our looks no longer sustain our place in the spotlight? Are we supposed to take our bow and go backstage as more youthful women take our place? Perhaps. However, if always being in the spotlight is important to you, you'll probably be

They pay a king's ransom to hold onto their youth.

the one splurging on the Botox and cosmetic surgery.

Looking older can throw you into a tailspin for a while. Get over it—your life's not over! Yes, the packaging may be a little worn, but perhaps the gift is still inside, especially if you've been too wrapped up in your appearance. It's time to have others look *to* you because they see your inner beauty instead of looking *at* your packaging. The research shows that older is better and with it comes many great surprises, such as the wonderful freedom of not caring anymore about what people think. Drop the stereotype of age and instead be true to yourself. How old do you feel when you are having fun and engaged in life? Exactly!

MY **EGO** SAYS

"I love to be wrinkle free."

MY *Spirit* SAYS

"I love that I'm free."

25

Shattered by Anger

Have you ever been with people who project anger? They may not be yelling and screaming, but the anger is palpable. It's as though resentment and hostility ooze from their pores; anger has become their essence. They can just erupt without warning. The slightest infraction can trigger an onslaught of insults and rage. It's as though their radar is set on sensitive, as they scan everyone and everything looking for potential offences. They assume attack

even when there's no one attacking. Angry people are often unaware of how their undercurrent of rage can create havoc and devastation in their lives— threatening relationships, destroying health, and robbing them of the enjoyment of life.

However, when expressed appropriately anger can be healthy; it's constructive, not destructive. Unfortunately, some of us learned to fear it instead. If showing anger was frowned upon when we were growing up, we probably learned to control and withhold our feelings, never learning how to express our anger in a healthy way. If we were raised in an atmosphere of yelling and abuse, we might now fear situations of conflict and strive to keep the peace at all costs. We choose to avoid anger rather than learning how to cope with it.

Others learn to wear anger like a suit of armor to protect themselves. They use intimidation and aggression to control those around them. Their message is "Keep away. I bite." Children learn what they live. Each of us copes in our own way, but the toxicity of unexpressed anger is like a deadly poison that festers inside, often leading to illness and addictions.

I grew up knowing when to duck—well, most of the time! My father's anger was often unpredictable. I remember hiding in the wardrobe when he'd erupt in outbursts of temper. When Mum would threaten to tell Dad, I took the threat very seriously. I have seen some of my dad's traits in myself and have brushed them off with the excuse that it's my hot Irish blood.

Angry people have their radar set on sensitive looking for potential offences.

Like most people, I'm not always rational when I lose my temper. My children remind me of an incident when I lost it with them. Parenting skills forgotten, it was not my finest hour of motherhood. Screaming like an Irish washerwoman, I chased them all around the house, lashing at their little legs with a dishcloth. They were terrified. Now they tease me about needing therapy for life!

I was relieved to learn that even though my childhood upbringing and genetic heritage bestowed on me a certain emotional temperament, this doesn't mean it's my destiny to be angry. I can change. I've discovered there are many ways to appropriately deal with feelings of anger and resentment. I can physically remove myself from the situation and decompress before I vent. Alone, I might shout and cry or even thump on a pillow. By retreating, I have time to rationally sort out the feelings and get to the bottom of what's really upsetting me. Some people like to write in a journal or talk about their feelings with a friend or counselor. For me exercise is one of the best ways to decompress. I walk or jog my feelings into a manageable state; as a bonus, I acquire much-needed endorphins to soothe my frayed emotions.

When your rage is disproportionate to whatever is going on, there is always something else fueling it. Anger is secondary to another emotion. Below anger are layers of fear, pain, frustration, or resentment; usually you're scared, hurt, or disappointed. The next time you're angry, take a moment to figure out what has really triggered your feelings. You might be surprised.

One of the most powerful and life-changing activities I facilitate in my workshop is an anger-release exercise. It's surprising to witness how much rage people hold inside. It's also shocking to some of the participants who, perhaps for the first time, get in touch with their hidden rage. It never ceases to amaze me how the women who appear to be the meekest and best mannered are often the most vocal in this process.

The exercise starts with participants bashing a chair with a plastic baton. This physical movement, "the tantrum phase" of the exercise, helps release unexpressed emotions locked in their tissues and cells. At the same time they use their voices to scream, yell, and cry. Yes, it gets

When your rage is disproportionate, there is always something else fueling it.

noisy—like in a delivery ward! Afterward, everyone works through a dynamic question process that involves six phases. It assists them in moving from anger to talking about their hurt, their fears, their regrets, and what they wanted or want from the relationship.

We conclude the process with an exercise in forgiveness. This purgative and cathartic process gives birth to a changed life for many of the women, as it clears the way for their healing to begin. I have witnessed some of the most "holy moments" of my career amid the heart-wrenching primal screams.

Only when the anger is gone can the healing begin.

MY EGO SAYS

*"I'm so angry
I want to hurt you."*

MY *Spirit* SAYS

*"I am hurt,
therefore I'm angry."*

26

Too Much Information

When I was a student I read books, pulled out the encyclopedias, or went to the library when I needed to research a topic. Now, like most people, I connect to the Internet to conduct my research. Within seconds I can acquire information from a multitude of sources. In a matter of minutes I have the latest facts, the most recent studies, and the most advanced findings. With our lives already on overload, when does it all become too much? How can we possibly

cope with this tsunami of information?

A big part of information overload is that there is too little time to properly digest and understand it all. When I research a topic, I am overwhelmed with websites offering differing opinions. There are research papers, people pushing products, YouTube, and countless other resources. And let's not forget the blogs from all the ordinary Joes, only too happy to share their thoughts. This is when I wish I had never Googled the question in the first place. Because now, buried under a mountain of opinions and with little time to sort through it all, I am more confused than ever. Cell phones and emails have speeded up the way we communicate, but technology hasn't increased our ability to process information.

Take my own example. Many times I have sought information on various health issues. When I had problems with my legs aching at night, I decided to be proactive. Surely the Internet would have the

solution to my problem. In just a few minutes I had
my diagnosis. My ailment had a name—Restless Leg
Syndrome—and there were 101 opinions on how to
treat it. I downloaded an e-book that claimed it had
the remedy — eliminating salt intake was the key. I
searched the medical sites and was advised to take
Parkinson's medication to fix the problem. I learned
about mysterious creams
and pills and picked up facts
about lymph drainage. I even
read blogs from fellow
sufferers, whose advice
included hot baths, exercise,
and relaxation techniques. I found the information
confusing, vague, and often conflicting.

*With our lives already
on overload, when does
it all become too much?*

Drowning in data and hundreds of opinions, I was
still no closer to relief. Over a two-year period of
investigation, I met with doctors specializing in sleep
disorders, got prescriptions for Parkinson's

medication (which I refused to take), swallowed calcium and other supplements, had hot baths and massages, and even had the veins in my legs checked. After two years of sleepless nights, I now know that I don't have Restless Leg Syndrome. My self-diagnosis from the all-too-available Internet turned my life upside down, and I suffered from my ignorance. Eventually the proper diagnosis was discovered—my hormones were imbalanced. I am finally sleeping through the night. This illustrates how information can be too easily misinterpreted. Just because we want instant answers to our issues, should we be so quick to hit the search button?

It is sobering to think that our brains are limited in their capacity to cope, despite information bombarding us at an ever-accelerated rate. We cannot catch up or adapt quickly enough. Have you ever thought you had a brain disease just because of your inability to retain information? No, it's not Alzheimer's;

it's your biology! Your brain is drowning with input. It's little wonder we often feel stupid when we can't remember the name of the movie that we just watched. Even our ability to pay attention is undermined by a crammed lifestyle. On top of that, indulgence in the passive world of television and movies conditions us not to think.

We think we're so smart, but the truth is we are so informed that we can't be bothered to think! Look at the news media and how fast they cover topics just to keep our short attention span engaged. We don't have a chance to feel the full emotional experience of sad and bad news. It's little wonder our fundamental

Our ability to pay attention is undermined by a crammed lifestyle.

social skills such as empathy and compassion are falling by the wayside.

Instead of building your brain power, enhance your social circuit by making an effort to stay connected to others. Control the input being shoveled into your life before it controls you. Turn it off and take breaks from your consumption. Stay informed without obsessing, and start to notice how being overwhelmed with information negatively affects the quality of your life.

MY **EGO** SAYS
"Give me more and I will be smarter for it."

MY *Spirit* SAYS
"Give me less and I will be the wiser for it."

27

Green with Envy, Red with Shame

I had never seen a more beautiful doll. Her shiny curls framed her perfect face; her eyes closed when she was laid in the pram, wrapped snuggly in her pink blanket. The teacher announced that the doll and pram were part of a charity raffle. Some lucky girl would win this prize. My stomach felt hollow at her words. I just *had* to own that doll. In my mind I was already playing house, pushing my new pram around the neighborhood to the envy of my friends.

My classmates started bringing in three-penny bits and even six-penny pieces, excitedly collecting their tickets, but I wasn't going to let them take my dolly. I sneaked into my mother's purse and removed a five-pound note. In those days a five-pound note would have bought a full basket of groceries; my plan collapsed when the teacher questioned my

cc

It's amazing the lengths we go to when we're lusting after something.

mother's incredible generosity. The shame was bad enough, but the loss of my doll to a beaming Catherine McKee was unbearable. I was so envious!

It's amazing the lengths we go to when we're lusting after something. We suffer envy when we covet what someone else has. We wish we had it and the other person didn't. She has a perfect figure and can eat anything and not gain an ounce. You hate her! She got the promotion you applied for. You'd like to celebrate her good fortune but you can't; your envy won't let you. Instead, through a fake smile and gritted teeth you say, "Congratulations Lisa," while visualizing a micromanaging boss and death by overwork.

It's normal to occasionally have envious thoughts, but we suffer when we allow ourselves to be green with envy. This happens when our envy becomes more than an occasional thought, when we start to change our behavior because of envy. Rather than deal with our own feelings of insecurity, we project our disapproval and even condemn those who appear to have more than we have.

Envy destroys relationships and drives fiscally prudent people into debt.

Envy can be especially insidious in relationships. People who are burning up with envy will often hide their feelings, but under the camouflage of the relationship they will undermine and covertly attack their rival. At the outset, the relationship may have the illusion of being healthy. The victim may not even be aware of the envious claws in his or her back.

This happened to me many years ago. A co-worker and I had collaborated on many projects, and it had felt like we were a good team. But something had changed, and for some reason she began to perceive me as a threat. As I listened to her dissension and even agreed to changes in the project, I felt belittled and defensive. Instead of the usual give and take in our relationship, it became a competition. She would be congenial and smiling to my face, but would make underhanded remarks about me to my colleagues. Finally a friend pointed out the obvious: "She's envious of you."

Envy can destroy relationships between co-workers and drive fiscally prudent people into debt to keep up with the Joneses. It can also send normal, reasonable women into plastic surgery.

Rather than suffer from what you think you lack, use your envy to show you what you want. It can be a smaller waistline, a better job, or even a beautiful doll wrapped in a pink blanket! Instead of allowing envy to feed your jealousy, use it to motivate you to work harder to get what you desire.

Catherine McKee didn't get to show off her new prize for long. It was reported that her little sister had poked out one of the doll's eyes. I know exactly how she felt.

MY **EGO** SAYS

"I want what you have."

MY *Spirit* SAYS

*"I admire what
you have."*

28

Too Nice for Your Own Good

I'll never forget the first time I said no with conviction. This occurred during my learning-to-be-assertive phase. Beside my phone, I'd placed a laminated card showing the graphic of a large red stop sign, but instead of the word STOP in the center, there was a huge NO.

This was my reminder to say no, just in case I lapsed into my old yes-saying ways.

John phoned me from the church that afternoon, confident that I'd agree to his request. After all, he, like everyone else, knew me as an "easy touch." There was a charity fundraiser to be organized, and the decision was unanimous—I was voted the best person for the position. He finished with the question, "So, Fran, what do you say?" I said no. The silence hung between us. John was so flabbergasted he couldn't speak. As I waited for his recovery I thought I'd die of guilt. And of course if I did die, I knew I'd be going straight to hell, because how can you say no to God's work? Eventually I got over the angst and the guilt.

I realized that my old "doormat" ways had given me the recognition of always being nice, helpful, and accommodating. The payoff was to be liked and loved by all. I might as well have lain on the floor and announced, "Go ahead, run all over me, wipe your feet—twice!" Instead of disappointing others, I would end up disappointing myself. I didn't like saying yes, when I wanted to say no.

Before I could begin to exercise my no-saying muscle, I had to learn to separate my feelings from everyone else's. As a yes-sayer, I'd automatically take on everyone else's feelings and negate my own.

I knew John really wanted and needed help for the church function, but for once I wanted to show up and enjoy the event without any responsibilities. What I needed to do was first

The payoff is to be liked and loved by all.

internalize the fact that I was worthy, then realize that what I felt and wanted was just as valuable as what others felt and wanted.

Another thing I needed to learn was what I want. When I was unclear on what I wanted, everyone else's wants took priority. I needed to take the time to clarify the outcomes I desired. Have you noticed that the people with the clearest goals usually get what they want? I started prioritizing my values and what mattered most to me. The family dinner hour was important to me, so I began protecting it. Then it became easier to say no to anything that might interrupt this valuable family time. I unplugged the intrusive telephone and refused to schedule anything between 6 and 7 p.m. I gave up an early evening gym time and rescheduled it for later.

Learning to say an honest no takes courage and a commitment to integrity.

I also needed to learn to be absolutely honest and clear on my motives when I did say yes. Did I really want to say yes or was I capitulating because I was afraid of being judged? Was I giving in because I would lose their approval? Was it an honest yes? Once I was clear on why I was agreeing, I was also clear about any hidden agendas that I might have.

Realize that the minute you begin to say no to what others want and yes to what *you* want, your inner critical voice will call you all sorts of names, like selfish, unloving, and mean. A whole paradigm shift needs to happen to move from self-rejection to self-respect. It doesn't happen instantly.

Learning to say an honest no takes courage and a commitment to integrity. Doing this honors you and it honors others. It gets easier with practice. Other people will learn to trust you and more importantly, you will learn to trust yourself. Is it worth it? Totally! I would rather disappoint you with a no than lie to both you and me with a dishonest yes.

MY **EGO** SAYS
"It's my way or the highway."

MY *Spirit* SAYS
"Accepting that we have differences is the higher way."

29

Facebook or Face to Face?

Like most people, I enjoy taking a break from the reality of life. By escaping for a few hours in a good movie or the pages of a great novel, I can easily disengage from the responsibilities and obligations of everyday living. But I've noticed a more disturbing kind of disconnection going on around me—people no longer wanting to engage and connect with each other.

I find myself doing the same. I will often choose to send an email rather than pick up the telephone. Email is easier and faster. It's more comfortable for me to send money to help dig a well in an African village than it is to get my hands dirty helping my neighbor with his lawn. I used to be active volunteering in the community; now I prefer to be passively entertained watching some reality show.

I've also noticed it's becoming more and more difficult to get people together for a social event. I used to think it was all about busy schedules, and yes, that's a problem. However, I think there is something more subtle and significant going on.

I heard recently that babies as young as six months old are being introduced to computer programs geared to enhance their brains. At a stage when it's crucial for children to develop social skills, instead we are introducing them to technology. We want to raise intelligent children but at what cost? Our youth are restructuring their brains playing games in a virtual world instead of developing their personalities and communication skills in the real world. Neuroscience has shown that this restructuring of the brain can result in a disconnection between actions and consequences.

Technology is only one aspect of this multifaceted problem. Many of us are becoming desensitized to the needs of others. If any commitment to help might be a burden or a sacrifice to us, we quickly shut off our empathy switch and disconnect. I believe it's time to wake up to what is going on all around us. This disconnection and isolation we're experiencing is changing us as a human species.

We don't seem to notice what is happening to us, and we don't want to notice what is happening to others. After all, we can barely keep our own lives together. What are we pretending not to notice?

In our hi-tech, low-touch world, I believe it's more difficult to sustain a healthy family life than it is to sustain a robust economy. Do you struggle to schedule weekday dinners with your family? Reality shows on TV often focus around large families who seem to have time to eat together. What's your family's reality? Do you gather around the kitchen table or disappear to eat in front of your individual computers?

As challenging as it is to schedule family time, it is even more difficult to stay connected with the community. Think about your neighbors. Are they essentially strangers you wave to on the rare occasion when you happen to back out of the driveway at the same time? You may have been living side by side for years, but how well do you know them? Too many people think they are engaged in life but are in reality living separate lives, disconnected from others and too busy to care.

Many of us are becoming desensitized to the needs of others.

Many of us prefer Facebook, Twitter, and text messaging to any face to face communication. Some of us are like robots, wired into our devices but tuned out of life. It's as though we have been hypnotized to accept that this is the way we "do life" today. After all, a virtual community is easier to manage because we can disengage without commitment. We simply log out. However, too much time spent in virtual experiences creates a shallow pseudo-community at the expense of real life interaction. What needs to change?

> *Some of us are like robots, wired into our devices but tuned out of life.*

When we take the human element out of our communication, we're losing an essential need to engage with each other. This cannot be duplicated in a virtual world.

Our son lives in Costa Rica. We use Skype, with our cameras hooked up to stay connected. I am grateful

that I can see his face and sense his well-being as I chat with him over the digital highway. I am grateful for this technology, but it can never substitute for sitting down and talking to him face to face, with our hearts and Spirits connected.

Ask yourself this: If you blocked your text messages and unplugged your computer, would your life be any different? Would you make the effort to connect with your friends or family? Would you drive or take the bus to meet with them? Technology is here to stay, but is it supposed to enhance or enslave us?

What if we are all walking toward a cliff and like lemmings we dutifully line up to go over the edge. Of course the reality is, no one will know or care that we're gone; they'll just notice that we're not answering our cell phone!

Instead of ignoring this problem, choose to become part of the solution. Shut down your computer and walk with a friend. Take the time to lean over the fence

and chat with your neighbor. Turn off the television and talk with your partner. Find a healthy balance between your virtual connections and those of the face-to-face kind.

Facebook or face to face; it's your choice.

MY EGO SAYS

"Plugged into social media is being connected."

MY *Spirit* SAYS

"True connection requires much more."

30

Sisters in the "Hood"

I always wanted to be the mother when I played house as a little girl. After all, the mom got to be the boss of the children. In my late 20's, when I finally became a mother myself, I had expectations that motherhood would be the pinnacle experience of my life, my crowning glory. And like everything else I put my mind to, I was going to be the best mother ever.

My innocent approach to motherhood was rudely adjusted as reality set in. I soon discovered life was wet and messy, like the barf on my new carpet, pee in my eye, or a leaky diaper on a neighbor's plush sofa. I'd manage to fake a smile behind my maternal mask, but sometimes all I wanted to do was hide and cry my eyes out. I worried that I was lacking some essential maternal gene because sometimes I actually looked forward to banishing my toddlers to a time out in their rooms.

Mothers are simply not supposed to feel bad about motherhood.

I'd drag my weary body to bed at night unable to stay upright for another minute, asking "Where did my life go?" Recalling the high-pitched temper tantrums at the grocery store and Crayola all over everything, I can't believe I ever thought motherhood was being the boss of anything.

Mothers today are expected to know everything, from how to raise responsible children to successfully removing a virus from the family computer. They work, volunteer, chauffeur, do endless errands, clean, shop, and still manage to cook a healthy meal—at least some of the time. They are amazing multi-tasking, self-sacrificing women who even remember what sexy means—well perhaps once or twice a year when they have some energy to spare!

The reality is that raising a family today can be a huge challenge. Not every mother copes as well as she'd like to. And yet, mothers are simply not supposed to feel bad about motherhood. This is an offence of the worst kind, a violation against nature itself. If you do complain, those apron-wearing, cookie-baking types might attack you. At the very least, you'll feel bruised by your own guilt. Aren't you supposed to be happy being a mother?

Sisterhood unite! We need to support, not judge, each other. Whether we stay at home to be with our children, raise them while we go to work, or decide not to have a family at all, we need to respect each other's choices. Life can be exhausting enough without having to defend our position.

I'm glad I was the mother; my husband wouldn't have survived for more than a week! So it wasn't always fun and it didn't always bring out my best side, but I did it. Just because motherhood is an important role doesn't mean you need to set unrealistic expectations; mothers raise the bar too high and then feel they're always falling short. Stop being so hard on yourself. No, you won't send your child into counseling for life just because you lost it!

Mothers, know you are not alone if you feel inadequate, exhausted, or if you dream of running away to Greece. I ran a mothers' group and taught parenting skills for a few years after my children were born. The learning was important, but by far the biggest benefit for the moms was when they talked among themselves and related to each other's experiences. Get out and meet each other; it's intoxicating and supportive to have another grown-up to talk to.

Hats off to all you moms out there! As a graduate of the school of motherhood, I can tell you it's worth it. Today I

Mothers raise the bar too high and then feel they're always falling short.

can say that with conviction, now that I've survived and caught up on my rest. Then again, the mother role is never really over; I'm tethered to my children until…

For every mother I suggest a special place in heaven for all your sacrifices, and of course to put your feet up for a while, like eternity! And take heart; the many rewards of motherhood do show up along the way. For me, the prize is in witnessing two incredible young adults who are confident and enthusiastic about their roles in life. They grew up well despite my shortcomings. It is an honor to be their mother.

MY EGO SAYS
"I am the mother; you honor me."

MY *Spirit* SAYS
"To mother is an honor."

31

Hello Darkness, My Old Friend

"$\mathcal{H}$ello darkness, my old friend. I've come to talk to you again."

These thoughtful lyrics by Simon and Garfunkel are at odds with a world that prefers to embrace only the light. In fact, I believe most of us will do anything to avoid or deny the darkness. We grasp at gladness and push away grief. We celebrate birth and run from death. We medicate our addictions to avoid swallowing our pain. Yet, in their famous song, Simon and Garfunkel are suggesting we need to accept the darkness because it's an authentic component of life.

Everyone experiences darkness. Everyone has pain and sorrow. Yet how can darkness be a friend when all we really want is to be happy? We forget that the contrast of darkness and light cannot exist without each other, that we cannot see the stars without the darkness, that we cannot know joy without knowing sadness, and that often something must die before something else is born. When we refuse to fully embrace both the pain and the joy of life, we are denying life itself.

Waiting in the shadows of life's darkest moments are emotions like grief, despair, fear, and anguish. It's little wonder we don't want to enter in. We can attempt to alleviate our suffering or find hope in the adage that this too will pass. But it's best not to rush or reject the process. Pills may sedate you, but they won't heal your emotional wounds; and there's no white knight coming to your rescue. Don't fret, this is only life happening. In the pain are many hidden lessons and gifts that will be revealed later. This often unwelcome experience is your invitation to participate, where the only way out is through the darkness.

I've faced the darkness when life has humbled me and brought me to my knees, begging. There were painful life situations such as when my mother died, when I experienced rejection from a group of women who were in no mood to accept change, and when I was told I had less than five years to live. Each of these experiences plummeted me into that dark and lonely place. I've also unwittingly sent myself to that dark place when I have refused to deal with my unexpressed anger and when I have ignored life's call to make changes.

Everyone experiences darkness. Everyone has pain and sorrow.

I used to always react negatively to life's hurts; in fact, I had two stances. The first was with both fists up as I defied life to take me down. The other stance was that of the sniveling victim, claiming that life wasn't fair. Of course, neither stance taught me anything because I was looking outward and not inward, blind to what I needed to learn and what I needed to heal. After all, I was in control and I had all the answers. Or so I thought. Now I know better. Instead of always trying to resolve everything by myself, I accept the invitation to go to that dark place. I willingly sit with my distress and ask for wisdom. Time and time again, what usually starts as a mindful and emotional process culminates into amazing spiritual growth.

Willingly sit with your pain and ask for wisdom.

I have been in awe at the wisdom revealed to me in those times of darkness. I would never have envisioned the path that has been illuminated nor the clarity that has been revealed. If it were not for the darkness, I would have missed the lesson of compassion for my broken self and the softening of my heart that had previously gone cold. My shame was fully felt when in that dark place a mirror was held up to reveal my need for control. My woundedness was laid bare in the shadows and I have been required to forgive myself and be forgiven, again and again.

The only problem with this process is that it's never on my time. I am often impatient as I wait and I struggle not to get busy checking emails or doing some other mundane chore.

You may have experienced your own dark night of the soul when, as F. Scott Fitzgerald said, "In a real dark night of the soul, it is always three o'clock in the morning, day after day." That's when life seems just too painful to bear.

I call this darkest of places the black hole. This is a frightening place, a gaping abyss, empty and pitch black; it has no bottom and no walls. I know because I have been there. In my dark night of the soul I

scrambled to reach for a handhold, anything to grasp onto as I fell further into the void. There was nothing there. I thought I'd die of fright. Down and down I plummeted until I felt I couldn't stand another moment of terror. And then it happened. Loving hands caught me. It was there in the darkness that I met God.

MY **EGO** SAYS

"I am all the light you need."

MY *Spirit* SAYS

"Hello, darkness, I'm here to see the light."

32

To Give Is To Live

When I was young, my mother tried to encourage character building through silent service to others. In my first character-building exercise I was to wash the dishes but was not allowed to mention that I did them or expect any acknowledgment for doing them. I don't think I lasted for more than a week. I just wasn't good martyr material!

My mother was a huge giver. She grew up in a generation that considered it honorable to offer help to anyone and everyone. Her generous Spirit flowed even though she was often tired and overburdened. I grew up with the message, "You give until you drop!"

For me, charity really did start at home.

I believe one aspect of the fallout of our increasingly disconnected and overburdened lives is that we are reluctant to share our limited time and energy with others, especially when we have a choice. I know I sometimes can't be bothered or I just haven't anything left to give at the end of the day. This is a dilemma, because life becomes hollow and worthless without the essence of generosity. It's an integral part of a meaningful life.

Winston Churchill said it best: "We make a living by what we get, but we make a life by what we give." Whenever we offer encouragement, donate money, volunteer time, or lend a helping hand, we are contributing something of ourselves. And when we give, the wonderful payback we receive is often much greater than any sacrifices we ever made. When we give everything and expect nothing in return, we receive joy, satisfaction, and happiness.

I had scrimped and saved for months to give my parents a trip to Hawaii as a surprise Christmas present. This was to be the ultimate gift, and I was feverish with excitement. That Christmas morning my sisters and I swayed our hips to Hawaiian music as we placed leis over Mum and Dad's heads. Mum laughed and shrieked, and Dad sat in shock when they realized what their surprise gift was. My joy was complete. The delight I felt for giving my parents their dream vacation was worth every sacrifice I had made to make it happen.

Life becomes hollow and worthless without the essence of generosity.

Unless we have a hidden agenda, the rewards of giving are always worth it. If our giving is really selfishness disguised as generosity, the rewards will never be enough.

It's amazing how we can be blinded by our own glow of goodness and remain unaware of the conditions tied to our contribution. Sometimes however, our agendas are blatantly obvious. The conditions of our generosity are clearly laid out for all to see; there are no subtleties. It's as though we give with one hand and hold out the other for our expected reward, such as when we volunteer to give a speech just to hear the applause and bask in the attention we know we will get. Or we send a gift to an acquaintance so they'll do business with us, or befriend a neighbor so we can get free babysitting. I suggest this is taking, not giving.

In every relationship—business or personal, casual or intimate—there's a flow of give and take. Balance is the key to keeping the relationship healthy. For example, if someone is a consistent taker in a relationship and doesn't balance taking with giving, the other person will soon begin to feel used and resentful. As Stephen Covey says, "Relationships are like emotional bank accounts: if you keep making withdrawals and don't make deposits, you'll soon be bankrupt." The same is true for givers. Givers also need to balance their giving with taking, or receiving back from the relationship. Many women have no problem giving but struggle with receiving.

Perhaps you can relate to this. Do you find it extremely difficult to ask for or accept help? Yet since you know the benefits and the joy of giving, wouldn't you also want others to experience that same joy by being able to give back to you? If you've been giving, giving, giving, and receiving little in return, consider that you may have unintentionally created a monster taker in the relationship. There needs to be a fair balance between giving and taking to keep your relationships healthy.

Can it possibly be wrong to give? Up until 10 years ago I would have answered with a passionate and unequivocal no. However, through my work with women and by closely examining my own behavior, I've now changed my mind. If I give because I'm afraid of being judged or rejected, or I give to avoid guilt or circumvent conflict, I am giving for the wrong reasons. If I am constantly jumping through hoops just to appease and please others, I am jumping through the wrong hoops. We all have reasons why we give; however, giving out of fear or guilt is a drain on our capacity to love and may result in resentment instead.

Many women have no problem giving but struggle with receiving.

I find it revealing to question my intentions before I give. Whenever I am offering a helping hand, buying a gift for someone, or even sending a card, I first ask myself what my intention is. I am always shocked if I discover my giving is designed to get approval. I may still choose to give; however, at least now I'm clear about my intention. This is an integrity issue for me. When I get clear on my motives, not only do I uncover any hidden agendas, I also reveal any expectations I might have.

On a recent trip to a blood donor clinic, I read the slogan "Blood—it's in you to give." I realized this applies not only to blood: I can give only what's inside me to give. We can give to others only to the extent we have looked after ourselves. When we have a healthy balance between being loved and loving ourselves, we have more than enough love and compassion left over to nurture others. When we are empathetic and compassionate, our giving flows effortlessly.

The most meaningful giving of all is when our generosity is free from any obligation and comes from deep within. This is a signal from our soul to give to another soul. We give and we receive. When we receive, we have even more to give—and so it goes. It's a perfect exchange. Teach this to your children. To give is to live, so give to your fullest measure.

MY **EGO** SAYS
"I give so that I'll get what I want."

MY *Spirit* SAYS
"I give without expectation."

33

Letting Go Never Ends

As a young mother, I clung tightly to my precious babies. "They're mine!" I declared. They were my priceless possessions, so I kept them close and never conceived of ever letting them go. When they started school, I stayed close by volunteering in the classroom, helping on field trips, and signing up for the PTA.

Eventually, when the time came to release my mother's hold on them, my heart ached with my loss. I stood on the doorstep as the white limousine pulled away, taking my daughter to her wedding—a smile on my face and an ache in my throat. She no longer needed me. I crushed my son close to my chest as I hugged him goodbye at the airport. I tasted my sadness in the salt of my tears. He no longer needed me. I felt cut off from life's flow, like a dead branch no longer viable. I watched from the sidelines with empty arms outstretched, calling, "Here I am, don't you need me still?" But I was alone in limbo and no one was coming.

Throughout life we are required to let go over and over again.

I eventually got over my dramatic despair; now I guard the door in case they want to move back in!

Do you have difficulty letting go? As babies, we have amazing grasp reflexes, but throughout life we are required to unfurl our fists and let go, over and over again. In our insecure world where fear is the boss, many of us are white-knuckling it through our days, snatching, grasping, and protecting what is ours. There are hundreds of ways we insist on holding on, even when the consequences are detrimental to our well-being and a burden to our health.

The stock markets fall, our security is at risk, and consequently we hold on tighter than ever. We hoard our stuff and are preoccupied with our possessions.

We cling to our youth, hang onto our looks, and pay a ransom to lift and tuck out of sight anything that is old. We obsess about weight, wrinkles, and worry lines and fearfully purchase a few more years just to remain youthful for a little longer.

We hold onto our anger when we've been wronged. Our indignant Egos claim the right to blame and judge. Anger held hostage remains locked in our cells, pacing and waiting for release.

With death we are forced to let go of our loved ones; it's a painful parting when the veil of death removes them from our grasp. This is the ultimate act of letting go. With death we have no choice. But daily we are faced with smaller deaths, where the choice is ours to release and move on.

Are you ready for something different in your life? Chances are you've been ready for a long time and yet you still haven't made a move. Why is that? Perhaps it's because you need to let go of the old first before you can embrace the new.

I have witnessed many women struggling because they insisted that life had to be a certain way. With determined minds, they resisted, persisted, and continued to push their lives uphill. Only when they ended their struggle and finally let go did they realize they were on the wrong path to begin with. Life isn't supposed to be such a hardship; in fact, life will support you when you surrender your Ego. Letting go is as essential to life as the very act of breathing. Do you hold on to your breath and hold on and hold on? Of course not, and yet you forget this truth when it comes to releasing things in life.

As I reflect on my own life, there have been many occasions when I have let go. I let go of my need to change my father and changed my heart instead. I gave up the desire to control every aspect of my life and have learned to trust instead. I relinquished my grasp on my children and I watched them fly from the nest.

The secret to life is to hold on lightly, love greatly, and allow life to follow its course, because letting go never ends.

MY EGO SAYS
"I can't let go."

MY *Spirit* SAYS
"Letting go is living freely."

34

Waiting for My Happiness

I thought when I got married my husband would make me happy. After all, that was his responsibility, right? Apart from being a provider, friend, lover, and father to my children, he was also supposed to keep me happy and content in our marriage. Then when I believed he was falling short of my happiness quota, I would blame and complain.

It wasn't until I was in my thirties that a counselor told me that no one else could make me happy. Happiness had to come from inside myself.

From inside myself? I had a hard enough time with the outside stuff without having to dig around in the dark looking for something that I didn't quite get! I didn't know how to *do* happiness. I didn't know how to *go* within. Yet it seems most of the good stuff comes from within—like inner peace, inner spirit, self-esteem, intuition.

I noticed that other people seemed to come by happiness naturally. Not me. Happiness was always elusive, hard to grab, slippery at best.

Sometimes a lack of happiness can be attributed to faulty filters. I grew up in a negative environment, in a world where the glass was always half empty. Consequently, I am the one who noticed the smudges on the window instead of the beautiful scenery. I would obsess about a problem instead of focusing on a solution. My husband, being a positive thinker, has helped me to see my negative programming. To change,

Happiness needs to come from inside.

I started to become vigilant about my perceptions. I guarded my thoughts because I knew they had the power to make my life heaven or hell.

Negative thoughts aren't the only thieves of happiness. Feelings of envy, greed, guilt, and fear are also culprits. Not living in the moment also robs us of happiness. The concept of living in the moment has been around for eons, even though our generation is just awakening to its truth. Happiness can be found in the moment, any ordinary moment. Not just the *Happy Birthday* or *Congratulations* type of moments but in the ordinary (and often extraordinary) moments of everyday life—such as taking the time to enjoy a freshly brewed coffee on a weekend morning, catching a magnificent sunset after a rainy day, or feeling a baby's hand cupped around your finger. Sadly we miss out on most of these everyday varieties because we are too busy, with heads bent to the wind—and get this— looking for happiness! We are never really *here* because we are always striving to be *there*, wherever there is.

The words *happiness* and *success* are often bandied about in relation to each other. Personally, I think you're a success if you are happy. I'm not as confident in the belief that if you become successful you will be happy.

It's the same with possessions and relationships. We are conditioned to believe that a beautiful home, a trendy wardrobe, or a love relationship will sustain our happiness. All too often, even when we get the things we think will make us happy, we are left unfulfilled and unhappy. We pull out all the stops. We work longer and harder to be happy some day, only to discover we could have been happy along the way. Happiness isn't a destination on a map or an object on the horizon. In fact, if you think about the horizon, what happens when you walk towards it? It moves away; you can never reach it. Happiness is not *out there*; it's *in here*—inside each of us.

I frequently ask women, "What would make you happy?" Too often they hesitate or look at me with a blank face. This confirms the fact that many women live life for everyone else. Consequently they forget who they are, never mind knowing what they want. Can they tell me what they dream about? The hobbies or interests they are passionate about? Sadly no.

So ask yourself the question, "What makes me happy?" Not your partner, not your children, not your boss—*you*. The more specific you can be, the more likely you will attain it. You've got to claim it to own it. It's imperative that you really get to know who you are, what's important to you, and what makes you unique, because authenticity is one of the keys to happiness. From personal experience I have discovered that the more true I am to myself, the happier I become.

Can we ever sustain happiness? Maybe if we stopped expecting our outside circumstances to satisfy our inner cravings. Perhaps if we ceased compromising our values and filled our days with what really matters to us. Maybe if we slowed down enough to appreciate simple pleasures in the moment and enjoy the serenity that comes from just being who we are.

MY **EGO** SAYS
*"When I'm
successful,
I will be happy."*

MY *Spirit* SAYS
*"Being happy
is a success."*

35

Laughing Out Loud

When was the last time you let out a rip-roaring belly laugh? Perhaps, like me, you realize it's been a while. With the approach of each new year, my husband consistently asks, "What would make this year better than last year?" And every year without fail I have the same answer: "I want more fun and more belly laughs."

Unfortunately, organizing time for some fun is relegated to the to-do list, along with getting my nails done, booking a colonoscopy, and picking up the dry cleaning. Getting together with friends for fun takes serious planning, especially when you need to schedule get-togethers weeks in advance. It's absurd! Here we are as adults making play dates for ourselves just to create some levity to temper the insanity of our busy, over-scheduled lives. Where does spontaneous playfulness fit into this culture we live in?

Let's have more fun and more belly laughs.

Have you ever heard a baby's belly laugh? It's hilarious—and so contagious. Or been around children when they have giggling fits? They know how to be silly and spontaneous. Not that long ago you used to be just like them. You began life fully equipped to have fun and laugh spontaneously. What happened? Life became the serious business of stresses and schedules. For many people, becoming a responsible adult meant suppressing formidable childlike roots and forgetting how great it was to play, have fun, and laugh.

Have you noticed the different ways people laugh? I shriek and am often heard above everyone else. Other people will crank out loud guffaws. Then there's the laugh-snort combo—a family member does this one to perfection. How about the knees-crossed-trying-not-to-lose-bladder-control laugher, the side holder, or the floor roller? Then we have the tittering tee-hee-ers, the tears-down-the-cheeks laughers, and the hee-hee leg slappers—that's my son. Laughing is contagious good fun.

Comedians do a phenomenal job exaggerating the absurdity of everyday situations that we find ourselves in. We laugh and howl at how ridiculous we can be. Wouldn't it be great if we could have the same perspective as we go about our day? Life is full of great comedic material if we would just lighten up. I understand it is often difficult to see the humor in the moment, especially when we're in a stressful situation. But later we can often look back and laugh at ourselves. Humor is also the best remedy for an uptight Ego.

Picture the time I noticed a familiar couple browsing the cereal isle in my local supermarket. We had enjoyed a fun evening together a few months previously. I launched my cart in their direction, waving and calling "Yoo hoo!" As I drew closer I realized to my horror, but much too late, that I didn't know them after all. There I was facing two very puzzled but smiling strangers, one holding a Shreddies box. Because my approach was so effusive, the brilliant actress that I am took over, and with conviction carried on talking, expounding on the wonderful evening we'd had together. We parted ways with me bolting out of the store vowing not to return for at least a century and them still meandering the isles wondering if I should

have been let out unsupervised! Sure, I can laugh at myself now, but it took a while.

Laughter is therapy; it's good for us. It connects us with others and is highly contagious. By laughing more we can affect those around us to laugh more too. This reduces everyone's stress levels and helps us release health-enhancing hormones. Having a good laugh also helps to lower blood pressure and releases oxygen to the brain. Whether we're belly laughing or just tee-heeing, laughter gives us a great internal workout and provides us with a physical and emotional release; it helps us decompress and let off steam. Laughter really is the best medicine. Instead of just popping pills to reduce our stress or build our immune system, we should be prescribing a daily dose of laughter.

From my couch I watch those TV commercials with the beautiful people laughing and having a jolly old time. As I sit in my fuzzy slippers and sip my herbal

tea, I often feel like a dull doormat with no life. Too often I am hoping "rent-a-crowd" will invite me to a party where the fun, the food, and the cleanup afterward, isn't my responsibility. It's too easy to become lazy and apathetic about socializing and creating opportunities for some good laughs. However, unless I make an effort, I become as boring and flat as the old soda pop that I bought for a party that never happened.

This year I have taken charge and upped my belly laugh quota thanks to my fabulous friends who allow me the freedom to be my silly self. The best nights out are the ones where my mascara has run, the knee crossing has failed, and I'm still laughing days later.

Laughing connects us with others and is contagious.

Laugh, lighten up, and allow yourself the freedom to be silly and foolish. Don't give a hoot about who may be watching you. They're all too busy anyway. Look for opportunities to inject humor into every day and get together with people who enjoy the lighter side of life and love to laugh. Life's too short to be serious; it will be over before you know it, and that's no laughing matter!

MY EGO SAYS
"I can't look foolish."

MY *Spirit* SAYS
"You're only foolish if you can't laugh."

An Encouragement

I hope that you've found value and meaning in reading this book; I did, after all, promise that there was a gift inside. Your take-away could be as monumental as a major life change or as small as a seed of insight. Or perhaps you have no idea yet what you've learned, but at least you've enjoyed the time out and a chance to put your feet up for a while.

When people ask me why I wrote this book, I tell them the truth. My Spirit put me up to it. Of course, my Ego tried to sabotage this project from day one and attempted to shut me up throughout the whole writing process. I had many long days when I couldn't write and nights when I couldn't sleep. That's when my Ego suggested that my writing wasn't good enough, proclaimed that I was going to be humiliated, and warned that it just wasn't safe to be vulnerable. If it weren't for my Spirit's persistent prodding, you would not be holding this book today. This is another example of how Ego can stop us in our tracks.

Maybe reading this book has given you a new way to look at life. Perhaps for the first time you have become aware of the choices you face daily to follow either your Ego or your Spirit. I know life is difficult enough without having to slow down and think about your choices. However, to be truly engaged in life takes a concentrated effort, and we need to be awake to new possibilities. Most women are asleep to the powerful influence of Ego and Spirit. They continue to react to circumstances while chained within the confines of an Ego-driven life. I encourage you to be different.

If you feel you have been sitting on the sidelines of life, isn't it time to join the parade? After all, feeling alive, connected, and engaged in life means involvement. Perhaps you are ready to tell your own stories, to connect with other like-minded women, or to finally follow your Spirit's leading. Just take a step, even a small one, and start marching. One doesn't define life by what you didn't do!

The degree to which you are authentic is the degree to which you feel alive. The world needs and deserves the authentic you. So step out, be yourself and realize just how fabulous you already are!

Who else do you know would enjoy *The Ego and the Spirit?*

Consider gifting:

~ Family & friends	~ Volunteer organizations
~ Women's groups	~ Business networks
~ Clients & customers	~ Church groups
~ Book clubs	~ Fundraisers
~ Sales & management teams	~ Annual conferences

For information on all Power of Focus products and programs go to: leshewitt.com

More Inspiring Books
for Your Library

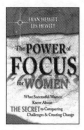

*The Power of Focus
for Women:*
How to live the life
you really want

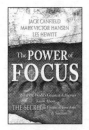

The Power of Focus:
How to hit your
business, personal
and financial targets
with absolute certainty

*The Power of Focus
for College Students:*
How to make college
the best investment
of your life

*The Power of
Faithful Focus:*
A practical Christian
guide to spiritual and
personal abundance

Available wherever fine books are sold. For more information,
visit www.hcibooks.com or call 1-800-441-5569.

Acknowledgments

Writing this book has been a labor of love, and I didn't do it alone. I would like to thank the many people who have contributed their talent and time to make *The Ego and the Spirit* a gift I am proud to share.

I am grateful to my readers panel who so graciously took the time to read the manuscript and share their feedback with me. A special thanks to Cyndy Watts, Melissa dos Ramos, Hildi Squirrell, Lynn Moerschbacher, Verna Masuda, Annette Stanwick, Farhana Dhalla, Jennifer Read Hawthorne and Liz Smith.

A special mention to my Artist's Way friends, Brenda Johnson, Rona Fluney, Lanice Jones, and Barb Lawrence. I feel honored to be part of such an inspired and gifted group. Thank you for your honesty, insights, and guidance. I hold you all in high esteem.

A big thanks to my sister-in-law, Caroline Alton. Your heartfelt feedback encouraged me at a point when I needed it most. To my wonderful sister, Anna, who through some miracle found the time to read the

manuscript. Anna, my heart is touched by your sacrifice and contribution. Thank you for your practical insight.

My incredible family is always a constant source of love and support in everything I do. Andrew, my amazing son, you are a lighthouse in my life. Thank you for your wise input.

Jennifer, my beautiful daughter, you continue to surprise me with a depth of wisdom beyond your years. Thank you my love for your effort—despite your overwhelming work schedule—and your invaluable comments to make this book even better. Also, thanks to my wonderful son-in-law, Ben, for his male input. Ben, I appreciate your authentic and intuitive ideas.

To Les—my love, my husband, my reader, editor, and encourager— thank you. These one-dimensional words cannot describe the depth of my appreciation for your continued faith and support in my work. Your unfailing commitment to our relationship and your loving devotion touch me to my core.

A special mention to my amazing editor and friend, Elissa Collins Oman, for her much-needed editorial skills, especially earlier in the writing process when my Spirit was in creative mode and the words tumbled out with abandon. So thank you, Elissa, for your guidance and your ability to understand the type of book I wanted to create. I am grateful for your faith in me and for honing and honoring the stories to reflect the message that I wanted to impart. Thanks also to Rod Chapman for his expertise and to Audrey Dorsch for her final edit. You have all contributed your invaluable experience, ensuring this book was a great collaborative effort.

A big thanks to Daniel Braha and James Burgin at Brandwithin Inc. for their wonderful graphic contribution to the cover and layout, plus their unrelenting patience when I needed time to reflect

and to make adjustments. Kudos also to Matthew Bennett for his amazing marketing expertise.

Lastly, and with a grateful heart, I give thanks to my Spirit for urging me to write. The book may be written but the work has just begun.

About the Author

Fran Hewitt is an internationally acclaimed author and personal coach who specializes in women's issues. Her authenticity and passion for helping others resonates with women from all walks of life.

Les Hewitt, her husband of 41 years, is the author of *The Power of Focus* book series. They reside in Calgary, Alberta, Canada.

To contact Fran, email: egoandspirit@shaw.ca